Foreword

As an affluent individual or head of a successful family, you've no doubt worked hard to create, grow and maintain your wealth. To get where you are today, you've had to overcome difficulties and make the most of opportunities. You should be proud of your accomplishments.

But the fact is, your job is not over. In coming years, you will almost certainly face more challenges—and more opportunities. That means you'll need to keep making smart choices about preserving and enhancing the wealth you have today so that it can help you achieve all that you want from life.

To maximize your chances for success, you will need two things.

First, you will need *a personalized and comprehensive strategy for managing all aspects of your wealth*—one that coordinates each piece of your financial life so that they all work together in concert. This will help ensure that your wealth is perfectly aligned with your core values and most meaningful goals so you and your family can live the life you want. The book you are holding, *The Wealth Management Edge*, outlines just such a strategy.

Second, you will need *a relationship with a caring financial professional who not only has the technical competence and knowledge to effectively serve as your personal CFO but also has the kind of life experience and perspective that will help you uncover and then achieve what's truly most important to you.*

Having worked in the financial services industry for nearly 30 years, I have learned how to delve deeply into my clients' backgrounds, relationships and passions to help them design a personalized wealth management plan that motivates them to accomplish their goals. I have also learned that while substantial wealth can be a great blessing, it can also be a great curse, so I work hard to help my clients and their children steer clear of the potential problems that often arise.

Impactful Real-Life Lessons

To help put my enthusiasm for *The Wealth Management Edge* in context—and to help explain my passion for providing my clients not just with comprehensive financial advice but also with a big-picture sense of what is truly important in life and how to achieve it—a quick review of my own family background and career path may prove useful.

My parents met during World War II in a Japanese relocation camp in Jerome, Arkansas. After two years, they were able to leave the camp to work and continue their courtship in Chicago. After World War II ended they were able to return to California, where they were married in the Hollywood Presbyterian Church. After my grandfather died, my dad returned to Hanford, California, south of Fresno, where I was born.

Fortunately, someone from the Hanford Presbyterian Church took title to my family's property when they were relocated and then transferred title back to them after the war. Growing up, I heard about this many times from the older generation—just as I regularly heard about what it took to get through the Great Depression—and in this way I came to understand the importance of being ethical and doing good things for others.

At the same time, since my family had a farm and a retail nursery business, I found myself drawn into the entrepreneurial aspects of business. After two years of junior college, I attended the Marshall

School of Business at USC and graduated with a BS in finance. I was out of college and already had been working in the financial services industry for about one year when my uncle passed away after his third heart attack. Along with my dad, he had been a huge influence on me, as both my uncle and dad sacrificed their own professional careers to take over the family business.

Unfortunately, because of my uncle's lack of estate planning, I watched my dad struggle with straightening out my uncle's various business and legal obligations. This made a big impression on me, and as an advisor it strengthened my interest in offering my clients a truly comprehensive approach. Several years later, after I moved to my current firm, I undertook the necessary coursework to obtain my CIMA® (Certified Investment Management Analyst) designation.

A Process for Avoiding Harm and Achieving Fulfillment

How do I know that the strategies, processes and general approach outlined in *The Wealth Management Edge* really work? The answer is twofold.

First, given my ongoing desire to serve my clients more comprehensively, I've always taken advantage of additional training opportunities, such as obtaining my CIMA designation. When I was first exposed to John Bowen and CEG Worldwide, I knew immediately that what they had pulled together over many years expressed in a powerful and elegant way what I was already trying to accomplish, and I felt that it would substantially benefit my clients. As soon as I could, I began implementing the various elements detailed in *The Wealth Management Edge*—including the importance of working with a team of experts on "advanced planning" activities as well as on wealth preservation, wealth transfer, wealth protection and charitable giving—and as a result, today my clients are working toward achieving greater levels of financial and personal success.

Second, I know that the ideas and processes detailed in this book really work because they are in complete alignment with my own values and philosophy—that is, with what's really important to me about being a financial advisor. Simply put, while I handle my clients' investments with great care and diligence, it's just as important for me to help them manage their wealth so that they and their families lead lives that are as meaningful and fulfilling as possible.

Above and beyond investments, then, my real focus is on helping my clients master the art of life. As James Michener put it:

> The master in the art of living makes little distinction between his work and his play, his labor and his leisure, his mind and his body, his information and his recreation, his love and his religion. He hardly knows which is which. He simply pursues his vision of excellence at whatever he does, leaving others to decide whether he is working or playing. To him he's always doing both.

Put differently, when you are my client, my focus is on your *personal fulfillment*—that is, the deeply felt sense that your life is full, whole and complete, and the knowledge that if you die tomorrow, your life will have made a real difference.

How do I help my clients master the art of life and achieve fulfillment? It all starts with a detailed "discovery" meeting where I ask new clients a set of 60 detailed questions designed to get at every aspect of their lives, from the financial to the personal, from the status of family members and pets to long-term goals and dreams.

I then apply the standard of the medical profession's great Hippocratic Oath—that in light of their needs, goals and dreams, my clients "do no harm" with their wealth. All too often, wealthy individuals have a dysfunctional array of investments, insurance products and outdated estate plans that make no sense at all given what's really important to them; therefore, I am keenly attuned to making sure that my clients' wealth is working for and not against them.

Our first step, then, is to sort things out and make sure that (to borrow from Stephen R. Covey) when they finish climbing the ladder of success, that ladder isn't leaning against the wrong wall. "How much is enough?" and "When is it enough?" differ for each client based on what will bring that person fulfillment, so by getting to the client's ultimate goals and values and working backward we can put into place a sensible big-picture cash flow and investment portfolio. We also look at what I call the "perfect calendar." If you had ample resources, how would you choose to spend your time, talents and efforts every day, whether in work, charity, hobbies or pleasurable pursuits?

"Do no harm" also comes into play with respect to passing wealth to the next generation. A shockingly high percentage of estates fail to transfer wealth in accordance with what was originally intended. Also, in far too many cases the presence of substantial wealth leaves the younger generation with what appears to be a strong sense of entitlement. I counsel my clients on the definition of tough love—*the key isn't what they want to give their children but what they want them to learn*—and we help put into place the kind of real-time budget and estate plan that encourage their children to become productive and fulfilled adults.

Conclusion

As someone who has lived a fulfilling life with many challenges, I prize nothing more greatly than assisting my clients in becoming aware of their own big picture so that we can optimize their financial situation to help them achieve what's most important. Whatever your focus may be—whatever will help you achieve fulfillment and master the art of living—you are much more likely to achieve your goals if you have a personalized and comprehensive financial plan in place that is overseen by someone who is experienced and committed to your success.

That's why I was so delighted to be asked to write a foreword for this book, because the concepts and strategies you'll find in *The Wealth Management Edge*, if taken to heart, can help you to profoundly change your life and the lives of those important to you for the better. I would be delighted to answer any questions that you might have about achieving your goals, and I wish you health, happiness and success in the years to come.

Stephen Takeda, CIMA®
Senior Vice President, Financial Advisor
Morgan Stanley Smith Barney LLC, Member SIPC

on the taxpayer. Clients should consult their tax advisor for matters involving taxation and tax planning and their attorney for matters involving trust and estate planning and other legal matters.

Bonds are subject to interest rate risk. When interest rates rise, bond prices fall; generally, the longer a bond's maturity, the more sensitive it is to this risk. Bonds may also be subject to call risk, which is the risk that the issuer will redeem the debt at its option, fully or partially, before the scheduled maturity date. The market value of debt instruments may fluctuate, and proceeds from sales prior to maturity may be more or less than the amount originally invested or the maturity value due to changes in market conditions or changes in the credit quality of the issuer. Bonds are subject to the credit risk of the issuer. This is the risk that the issuer might be unable to make interest and/or principal payments on a timely basis. Bonds are also subject to reinvestment risk, which is the risk that principal and/or interest payments from a given investment may be reinvested at a lower interest rate.

International investing may not be suitable for every investor and is subject to additional risks, including currency fluctuations, political factors, withholding, lack of liquidity, the absence of adequate financial information and exchange control restrictions impacting foreign issuers. These risks may be magnified in emerging markets.

Insurance products are offered in conjunction with Morgan Stanley Smith Barney's licensed insurance agency affiliates.

Trust and other fiduciary services are provided by third parties, including Morgan Stanley Private Bank National Association, a wholly owned subsidiary of Morgan Stanley.

Steven Takeda utilizes the services of CEG Worldwide.

Table of Contents

Building a Great Financial Life

"Let's face it—man's best friend is money."

I N LIFE, WHEN WE NEED TO GO SOMEWHERE WE'VE NEVER BEEN, IT'S a good idea to bring along the right road map. That's exactly what this book is—a road map that will guide you and your family to a lifetime of financial success, security and peace of mind.

In this book, you'll discover a way to manage your wealth—*the Wealth Management Edge*—that many of today's affluent families are using to help them live highly successful, deeply meaningful lives. By the time you have finished reading, you will see how to apply the very same techniques and strategies in your own life so you can go out and achieve all that is truly important to you and the people you care about most.

I know this because I have used the Wealth Management Edge to help thousands of investors enhance, protect and transfer their wealth. For more than 30 years, it's been my mission to help investors make the smartest possible decisions about their money and avoid the common pitfalls that trip them up, so that they can get all that they want from life. It's safe to say that I could not have accomplished that mission without the Wealth Management Edge.

For much of this time, I helped investors as one of the financial services industry's top financial advisors. Today, I coach other elite financial advisors on how they can help their clients use the proven steps outlined throughout this book to maximize the probability of achieving what is important to them. In working with hundreds of the top financial advisors and through them thousands of families, I've discovered clear patterns of success—the key *"do's"* and *"don'ts"* of managing wealth successfully. So I have complete confidence when I say to you: When it comes to managing wealth, the Wealth Management Edge works.

Capturing the opportunity

Before we go any further, let's acknowledge an important fact: You are one of the most fortunate people on the planet. As someone with wealth who was lucky enough to be born into a capitalist society, you are in an amazing and enviable position. You have the opportunity to have a hugely positive impact on your family, on other people you care about and even on the world at large. It's so easy to forget this fact given all the things we have to do every day, so take a minute to reflect on your good fortune.

But to make the most of the opportunities you've been given, you've got to make smart choices. You need to manage your entire financial life as best you can and act as a good steward of the wealth you possess. If you do that, your wealth will become a powerful source of good for you and those around you. Fail to do so, and you could easily and unnecessarily compromise your future and the future of many other people that you care about.

I have written this book to show you how you can identify what you and your family want most from life—and then go out and make it happen. My goal is to give you the knowledge, resources and tools that you need to manage your wealth so that you and your family achieve what is truly important to you.

The need for the Wealth Management Edge

The Wealth Management Edge is a step-by-step process that coordinates all the moving parts of your financial life so that they work together as they should to help you achieve your biggest goals.

The need to use this type of coordinated approach has become essential. Think about it: We all face more financial challenges than ever—from building and enhancing our wealth to protecting and passing it on to heirs to using it to support the people and institutions that we value most. What's more, none of these challenges exists in a vacuum. The decisions we make today about our investment portfolios, for example, can have far-reaching ramifications on next year's tax bill or the amount of money we are able to give to our children years or even decades down the road.

BUILDING A GREAT FINANCIAL LIFE

Wealth Management Edge strategies are based on the knowledge that the many and distinct areas of our financial lives are actually highly intertwined with each other and therefore need to work in unison.

As you can probably guess, the benefits of coordinating your entire financial life can be enormous. For example, one financial advisor whom I have coached discovered that a new client—an executive earning a six-figure income—had no estate plan of any kind, held insurance policies that were set to expire and worked with an accountant who was charging him huge fees to prepare very basic tax returns. By addressing each of these areas in a coordinated manner, the executive is now saving nearly $7,000 a year in accounting fees and has his assets positioned to minimize estate taxes down the road. In addition, his insurance is set up to ensure that there are no gaps in coverage that could expose his family to dangerous financial risks.

Just as important, however, are the substantial potential costs—financial, emotional and otherwise—of failing to manage your affairs in an integrated way. Consider another financial advisor I coached who works with an older couple. Both the husband and wife have adult children from previous marriages, and as a result, the couple wishes to keep their respective finances separate so that they can be sure that their own children will be taken care of according to their wishes. However, it turned out that many of their financial assets were actually co-mingled—such as a house they had purchased jointly. They mistakenly believed that the wife's children would receive 50 percent of the house's value and the husband's kids would get the other 50 percent. Instead, the titling of the asset ensured that the house would automatically go to the surviving spouse and then directly to that spouse's children upon the survivor's death—leaving out one side of the family entirely. Fortunately, their financial advisor discovered the situation and retitled various assets appropriately.

Take a minute to think about your own situation. Have you taken the time and effort to make sure that your entire financial house is in order—from investments to wills, trusts, insurance and other major issues—and that all the pieces fit together as they should? Or are there important areas of your financial life that could benefit from some attention and improvements? The fact is, despite our best intentions, the many demands of daily life tend to intrude and prevent us from doing what we know we need to do to ensure a great financial future.

If you know that you could be doing a better job managing your wealth—or even if you are the least bit uncertain about where you stand today, where you want to be in the future and how you'll get there—I encourage you to read on and see how the Wealth Management Edge can help.

Putting investors first

I realize that you may not have heard of the term Wealth Management Edge. That's not surprising. The Wealth Management Edge is part of an important evolution that is under way in the financial services industry—one that is resulting in fundamental improvements in how investors can make decisions about their financial lives.

I know this because I have seen this evolution firsthand and have even played a part in shaping it. I was a financial advisor for 16 years, working with many different types of investors—from young families just getting on their feet to extremely affluent executives in the Silicon Valley area and elite members of the entertainment and sports industries. One of the most striking things I learned during that part of my career was that nearly all the investors who came to see me had made costly financial mistakes at some point in their lives. It didn't matter if they had $50,000 or $100 million or more—virtually all of them did things with their money that made it harder for them to achieve their future goals and dreams. Worse, their mistakes would have been completely avoidable if they had just made a few simple moves. One of the most satisfying parts of being a financial advisor was helping my clients to get back on track financially so they could start achieving all that was important to them.

Unfortunately, the financial services industry I worked in didn't always make it easy for me to bring those benefits to investors' lives. When I first started out, the industry was strictly *firm-driven*. That means that the large firms that financial advisors worked for did all the research on financial markets and investments. This research was then passed down to the firm's stockbrokers, whose job it was to sell the firms' investment recommendations to clients so the firm could make lots of money. Under this firm-driven model, brokers—including me, I'm afraid—were little more than glorified salesmen. And our clients? They were more like customers who were there to be sold to instead of advised.

As someone who cared deeply about helping clients make the best choices about their money, I felt that this firm-driven approach was deeply flawed—especially when the firm's investment recommendations didn't pan out. When that happened (which was way too often, by the way), I would have to go back and apologize to my clients for something unexpected happening that resulted in them losing some of their hard-earned money.

Although I was a highly successful broker at the firm where I worked, I quickly became disillusioned by the seemingly constant stream of less-than-optimal products and advice we were giving to our clients—the very people whom we owed it to do right by! I had recently started teaching investment theory in graduate school at night, and after getting home from a class, I told my wife that I was thinking of quitting the business entirely to focus on teaching students.

Around this time, two turning points occurred that changed my life. The first was when my boss called me with big news: I had been named the firm's top financial advisor and was to be honored in front of my peers. I should have been happy, but my first thought was, "If I'm the top guy in the company and I'm this miserable, how are the rest of my co-financial advisors feeling?"

The second turning point happened during a class I was teaching about the methods that large institutional investors used to successfully manage their portfolios. One of my students raised his hand and asked me if I was using these same proven methods with my own clients. I admitted I wasn't, and he asked me why. I realized I didn't have a good answer for him.

These were "light bulb moments" for me: If Wall Street wasn't going to give investors the best possible advice and put their interests first, then I would do it myself.

I had found my calling—to fundamentally change the business model from firm-driven to *client-driven*, where the clients became the real bosses and everyone else worked for them. Under this client-driven model, the clients are at the top and the job of the financial advisors is to support their clients' true

EXHIBIT 1.1
FROM FIRM-DRIVEN TO CLIENT-DRIVEN

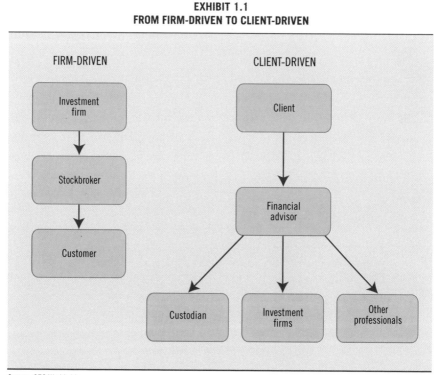

Source: CEG Worldwide.

needs and goals. They do so by having the freedom to choose the very best tools and resources available—from custodians to investment firms to other professionals that can help the financial advisors do a great job for their clients. (See **Exhibit 1.1.**)

In 1987, my two partners and I started a new financial advisory practice to help affluent families achieve their goals. I would no longer sell the products that a company wanted me to sell. Instead, I would work entirely on behalf of my clients by serving as their personal chief financial officer—helping them make the right financial decisions in all areas of their financial lives and working with other financial professionals as needed to address the full range of issues that each client faced.

This client-driven approach was the inspiration for the Wealth Management Edge. For the next 11 years, my partners and I brought the Wealth Management Edge to hundreds of families and helped them realize their dreams.

As we did this, financial advisors would increasingly ask me about my methods and how they could better serve their own clients. I began to see that financial advisors themselves lacked the right road map to success. Eventually I decided it was time to share my experiences with my peers. In 2000, after my partners and I sold our $2 billion-in-assets-under-management advisory practice, I created CEG Worldwide to coach financial advisors on how to deliver a world-class level of service and advice to their clients through the Wealth Management Edge.

I'm proud to say that through CEG Worldwide, more than 10,000 financial advisors have learned and implemented client-driven Wealth Management Edge approaches and are making a positive difference in their clients' lives. In the process, we are fundamentally changing how the financial services industry operates and delivers value to today's successful families.

And, yet, our work is nowhere near finished. It probably won't surprise you that much of the financial services industry is still clinging to its old, firm-driven ways and resisting the idea that the clients themselves are the real bosses. Indeed, our research shows that the Wealth Management Edge model has been adopted by just 6.6 percent of the financial advisors working today. The rest—93.4 percent—continue to treat investors as customers who should be "sold to" instead of truly advised. This is why the Wealth Management Edge isn't something you'll read about much in the popular financial press or hear about from your typical financial advisor. They don't practice it, and they don't want you to know about it.

My hope is that this book will help change all that by making the Wealth Management Edge approach available to more families so that they can achieve all that is important to them.

In the following chapters, I will walk you through the financial road map that the most successful families I have had the privilege of working with have used, so that you can bring that same level of success to your own life. Always remember that your good fortune comes with a price: You owe it to yourself, your family and your community at large to use your wealth to accomplish great things. I think you'll see that the Wealth Management Edge is the key to making those great things happen.

Now let's get started!

2

Confront Your Key
Financial Challenges

*"Have you given much thought to what kind
of job you want after you retire?"*

CONFRONT YOUR KEY FINANCIAL CHALLENGES

MOST OF US LEAD VERY BUSY LIVES AND FEEL AS IF WE ARE continually juggling multiple priorities and demands on our time. As you make plans for your future, it's important to take a step back from the all those daily responsibilities and really consider the road ahead. If you think about it, at the end of the day you are essentially the chief executive officer of your family. You are responsible for making the decisions that will determine whether you will achieve your financial dreams.

That means you need what every successful CEO has: a sound understanding of the obstacles you face and a comprehensive approach for overcoming them. To achieve financial success, you'll first need to get a handle on the biggest financial challenges that you'll encounter on your journey toward realizing all that is important to you and your family.

By recognizing the key financial issues you face, you will put yourself in the best possible position to make intelligent decisions about your money, create a plan that addresses these challenges in a coordinated manner—and, ultimately, live the life that you envision for yourself and your family.

The five major areas of financial concern

A few years ago, my firm's director of research at the time, Russ Alan Prince, conducted a study of more than 1,400 investors each with at least $500,000 in liquid assets. This landmark study was—and still is—one of the most comprehensive and relevant examinations ever done of the affluent and their financial concerns. For that reason, its findings have become the foundation of the Wealth Management Edge experience.

This extensive research tells us that the vast majority of today's affluent investors share the following five major key concerns about their financial futures.

Think about your own financial life as you review these top concerns. You may have additional issues that are unique to your specific situation, but chances are that many (and maybe all) of these challenges are at the top of your list.

Challenge No. 1: Preserving your wealth

Your goal with wealth preservation is to produce the best possible investment returns consistent with your time frame and tolerance for taking investment risks. As one financial advisor I work with likes to say, "It's not about how much you make; it's about how much you *don't lose.*"

Preserving wealth throughout one's lifetime has become the single biggest financial issue that most of today's affluent investors face. Just ask yourself this question: How sure are you that you have, or will eventually have, the wealth that is required to meet your needs, reach your various goals and live the life you want?

More affluent investors are asking themselves this very question, due to the severe market disruptions and uncertainty in recent years. In Prince's landmark study of more than 1,400 affluent investors, *nearly 90 percent* said that they were quite concerned about preserving their wealth. (See **Exhibit 2.1.**) What's more, the vast majority of investors—71.5 percent—said that they worry about having enough money to last throughout their retirements.

Remember that these are investors each with at least $500,000 in assets. Clearly, having significant wealth doesn't erase or minimize the fear of losing what you have worked hard to build up over the years. That makes sense. After all, there's simply too much at stake not to be concerned. The prospect of downshifting our lifestyles isn't the least bit appealing to most of us. And yet some affluent investors have found that they may need to make significant compromises to their future plans because they face the very real threat of failing to preserve their wealth.

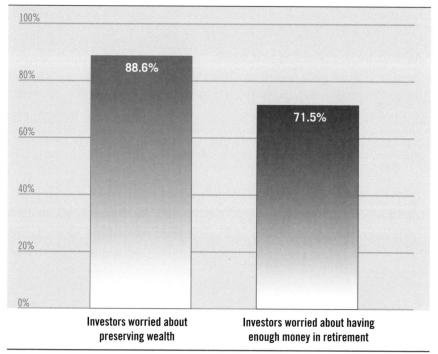

EXHIBIT 2.1
INVESTORS ARE VERY CONCERNED ABOUT PRESERVING WEALTH AND THEIR RETIREMENTS

Source: Russ Alan Prince and David A. Geracioti, *Cultivating the Middle-Class Millionaire*, 2005, Wealth Management Press.

There are numerous reasons for this predicament—some of which you may know about all too well. When most of us think about our net worth, the first thing that comes to mind is our investments. And the fact is, as investors we tend to make costly mistakes with our investment portfolios. Worse, we tend to make these mistakes over and over again. Huge volumes of research across multiple disciplines have proven that as human beings, we often let our emotions get the better of us when we make decisions about our assets—and that those emotional decisions cost us dearly in terms of lost wealth.

Consider, for example, that while the S&P 500 index returned 9.1 percent annually during the 20 years through 2010, the average investor in stock funds earned an annualized return of just 3.8 percent.[1] A big reason for that dramatic underperformance: excessive trading. Instead of adopting a buy-and-hold strategy, the average stock fund investor holds his or her funds for just over three years[2]—hardly a long-term time horizon.

If you're like most people, you don't think of yourself as an especially sophisticated investor. But I define a sophisticated investor as someone who has lost money in the financial markets at least once and did not enjoy the experience. By that measure, we are all sophisticated investors. We hate to see our net worth decline in value due to market volatility and our own errors in judgment. But for most of us, the thought of successfully sorting through the often confusing mix of investment opportunities, building a thoughtful investment plan and then sticking with it so it works as it was intended can seem extremely difficult if not downright impossible. That is why in Chapter 4 we will explore the foundation of a successful Wealth Management Edge plan—the investment consulting process.

There are numerous other hurdles in your path beyond choosing your investments—for example: inflation. You probably realize that, over time, rising prices of goods and services erode the value of your money and purchasing power. But have you ever considered how big inflation's effects can be on your financial comfort and security? Consider this: An annual fixed income of $100,000 would be worth just $86,000 in five years and only about $40,000 in 30 years, if inflation averaged its long-term historical rate of around 3 percent. Meanwhile, the amount of money you would need in 30 years to buy what $100,000 will get you today would soar to more than $240,000.

Often overlooked, inflation needs to be on your radar because it will have plenty of time to eat away at your wealth. That's because Americans are living longer than ever before, thanks to advances in health care. It's not at all unrea-

---

[1]Dalbar, *Quantitative Analysis of Investor Behavior,* 2011.
[2]Ibid.

sonable for a typical 65-year-old today to live for another 25 years or more. This is a great benefit of modern life, of course. But the downside is that you must make your money last much longer than your parents and grandparents did. That's a challenge that can seem especially daunting when you consider the potentially declining role of Social Security and pensions in the lives of the typical retiree, along with the rising costs of health care that seem to claim more and more of our savings each year.

Some of the challenges you face are new, while others have been with us for a long time. Regardless, many of these problems are gaining momentum each year—leaving even highly affluent families feeling more insecure about their future prospects than ever. In the wake of that uncertainty, it is absolutely crucial that you make the smartest possible decisions about your wealth based on the realities of the world.

Challenge No. 2: Mitigating your taxes

You also need to enhance your wealth by minimizing the tax impact on your financial picture. Taxes may be, as Franklin D. Roosevelt once said, "dues that we pay for the privileges of membership in an organized society." But that doesn't mean investors look forward to paying for those privileges.

Consider that nearly 85 percent of the affluent investors from the same survey cited above said that mitigating incomes taxes is one of their major financial concerns. In addition, mitigating estate taxes and capital gains taxes also ranks high on the list of affluent investors' concerns. (See **Exhibit 2.2.**)

Sound familiar? It's no surprise that so many of you share these tax-related concerns. Taxes can—and do—eat up a great deal of wealth.

Take income taxes. Many affluent families today have become successful by working hard and earning substantial incomes in the process. In fact, the incomes of high earners have grown far more rapidly over time than have the

EXHIBIT 2.2
PERCENTAGE OF INVESTORS CONCERNED ABOUT MITIGATING VARIOUS TAXES

Mitigating income taxes	Mitigating estate taxes	Mitigating capital gains taxes
84.7%	49.2%	41.7%

Source: Russ Alan Prince and David A. Geracioti, *Cultivating the Middle-Class Millionaire.*

incomes of lower earners. As a result, the affluent pay a significant percentage of all federal income taxes. For example, the top-earning 1 percent of Americans paid 38 percent of federal income taxes in 2008 (the most current data available as of the writing of this book), while the top-earning 5 percent paid nearly 60 percent.[3]

Taxes on investment returns also can have a big impact on the ability to grow and preserve wealth. From 1926 through mid-2011, for example, stocks

[3]Mercatus Center, George Mason University (mercatus.org/sites/default/files/publication/income-tax-equity-pdf2_0. pdf).

gained 9.9 percent annually. After taxes, however, that return fell to just 5.5 percent. Bonds' 5.5 percent return dropped to a mere 2.7 percent once taxes were taken into account. In real terms, a $1 investment in stocks back in 1926 would have grown, before taxes, to $3,159 by the middle of 2011—but just $97 on an after-tax basis.[4]

What's more, tax laws seem to be in an almost constant state of flux these days, with many investors worried that tax rates will eventually soar to help pay for the federal deficit. Obviously no one can be certain what the future holds when it comes to the government's decisions about tax rates and other aspects of the tax code. This uncertainty is preventing many families today from taking a proactive approach to tax planning.

This is a big and potentially very costly mistake. You cannot simply ignore the issue and wait for 100 percent clarity. You'll probably be waiting a long time if you do! Tax mitigation needs to be a key part of any financial plan for you and your family regardless of the political environment at any given moment in time. As the famous federal judge Billings Learned Hand once said, "There is nothing sinister in so arranging one's affairs as to keep taxes as low as possible." You can, for example, create a wealth management plan that has ample flexibility should the tax environment change for the better or the worse.

There are a number of strategies that can help mitigate both income and investment-related taxes, which we will explore in Chapter 5.

Challenge No. 3: Taking care of your heirs

Have you considered the legacy and financial resources that you will one day leave to your family? If so, you're not alone. Approximately 80 percent of affluent investors said that a major concern is ensuring that their spouses, heirs,

---

[4]Dimensional Fund Advisors (calculated using a combined federal and state marginal tax rate of 50 percent and a long-term capital gains tax rate of 25 percent).

parents, children and grandchildren are taken care of in accordance with their wishes and with minimal difficulty and cost. (See **Exhibit 2.3.**)

And yet, many investors aren't taking the appropriate steps to address this concern. The same survey discovered that the vast majority of these investors (a full 89 percent) have estate plans that are more than three years old.

Think about your own situation. Do you have a plan in place for passing on your wealth to family members, either now or down the road? If so, is it up to date and does it reflect current laws as well as your family's current and future needs, goals and level of wealth?

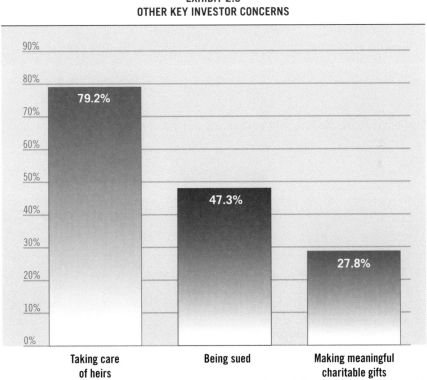

EXHIBIT 2.3
OTHER KEY INVESTOR CONCERNS

Source: Russ Alan Prince and David A. Geracioti, *Cultivating the Middle-Class Millionaire.*

CONFRONT YOUR KEY FINANCIAL CHALLENGES

The fact is, it is very easy to ignore this crucial concern because addressing it requires us to ask ourselves questions that we may not have ever considered—or that we might prefer to ignore. For example, how do you want your assets to be distributed at death? How and when should your heirs receive an inheritance? How can liquidity needs be met if your estate is illiquid?

These questions may create some discomfort. But let's face it: Failing to ensure that your wealth goes exactly where you want it to go can lead to much greater discomfort later on and have serious ramifications on everything from your ability to help your family members achieve their goals (such as a college education) to the long-term succession and sustainability of a family-owned business.

That's why families today need to be proactive in their wealth transfer planning efforts if they truly want their wealth to benefit their families to the fullest extent possible. In Chapter 6, you will find specific strategies for effective wealth transfer.

Challenge No. 4: Making sure your assets are not unjustly taken

Affluent investors don't just want to preserve their wealth against losses in the financial markets and guard against rising costs. They're also seeking to protect their assets from being unjustly taken from them by a catastrophic loss, potential creditors, litigants, ex-spouses and children's spouses, and even identity thieves.

Is wealth protection on your radar screen? Nearly half of the affluent investors surveyed are worried about being sued (see **Exhibit 2.3**)—not surprising, given how litigious our culture has become. This means that successful wealth management planning for many of you must address controlling risks through business processes, employment agreements and buy-sells, as well as restructuring various assets and considering legal forms of ownership—such as trusts and limited liability entities—that put your wealth beyond the reach of creditors and other parties who may seek to take it. You will learn more about these and other wealth protection strategies in Chapter 7.

Challenge No. 5: Donating a portion of your wealth

Increasingly, affluent investors are looking outward beyond their own families to the world at large. For these investors, making meaningful gifts to charity in the most impactful way possible is becoming a key issue. (See **Exhibit 2.3**.)

Charitable giving comes with its own unique set of challenges—from selecting the appropriate means of giving (such as direct gifts, donor-advised funds or private family foundations) to selecting causes and specific organizations that will have the biggest impact. Any gifting strategy you put in place should be set up for maximum effectiveness, of course. At the same time, however, you must ensure that your philanthropic objectives are in balance with your other key financial goals, such as retirement and the long-term financial security of your family. With that in mind, Chapter 8 focuses on successfully navigating the charitable planning process.

Coordinating your response

Now go back and review the list of the top five financial challenges. You will probably agree that each one taken on its own is daunting enough. But when you face many of these challenges and possibly even all five, as is the case with many affluent investors, they can have a huge impact on your ability to achieve a secure, comfortable and meaningful life. Again, that's because none of these five areas of concern stands in isolation from the rest. Wealth protection, for example, is often intertwined with wealth transfer needs. And charitable giving can often support goals in each of the other four areas.

Remember, all of the key areas of your financial life are tied together in ways both large and small. Plotting out strategies for just one area at the expense of the others is therefore a recipe for financial failure. To be most effective, you need to deal with each area systematically while also taking an integrated approach to your overall financial picture at all times.

The Wealth Management Edge recognizes these connections and provides recommendations that enable you to build a plan that addresses in a coordinated manner all of the challenges you and your family face. The end result: You gain control over your financial destiny and enjoy the peace of mind that comes from knowing that all the components of your entire financial life are working together as one well-oiled machine to get you to where you want to go.

In the next chapter, you'll see exactly how the Wealth Management Edge makes all this happen.

3

The Wealth Management Edge Approach

"No, not there, please. That's where I'm going to put my head."

THE WEALTH MANAGEMENT EDGE APPROACH

IN THE LAST CHAPTER, YOU LEARNED ABOUT THE KEY CHALLENGES that you and your family face on your path to financial success and comfort. Make no mistake: Addressing those sizable challenges is a major task—one that will take considerable effort and care to accomplish.

The good news: The Wealth Management Edge enables you to organize and manage your wealth so that all the components of your financial life work together toward one purpose—achieving the goals you most want for yourself, your family and your community. The Wealth Management Edge means having all of your financial challenges addressed and your entire financial situation enhanced. It goes beyond traditional investment ideas to encompass all types of financial needs throughout all the phases of your life.

Wealth management defined

What, exactly, is the Wealth Management Edge? At its core, the Wealth Management Edge is designed to address affluent investors' full range of challenges on an ongoing, long-term basis and coordinate all of the disparate aspects of wealth that you must address to build a meaningful life.

The Wealth Management Edge accomplishes this in three ways:

1. **Using a consultative process** to gain a detailed understanding of your deepest values and goals and your most important financial wants and needs.
2. **Using customized recommendations designed to fit your unique needs and goals beyond simply investments.** The range of interrelated financial services and tools might include, for example, investment management, insurance, estate planning, business planning and wealth protection.
3. **Implementing these customized recommendations in close consultation with your professional advisors.** The Wealth Management Edge en-

ables you to work closely with trusted advisors (as desired) on an ongoing basis to identify your specific needs and design custom approaches to help meet those needs.

Broadly, this process incorporates the three main components of the Wealth Management Edge, summarized in the following formula and discussed in greater detail below:

Wealth management (WM) = Investment consulting (IC) + Advanced planning (AP) + Relationship management (RM).

- **Investment consulting**—positioning your financial assets to achieve your goals, return objectives, time horizons and risk tolerance—is the foundation upon which any comprehensive wealth management plan is created. It is through investment consulting that you will address what is likely to be your most pressing financial concern: wealth preservation. The key investment planning concepts that you can use to guide the management of your investment portfolios will be explored in Chapter 4.
- **Advanced planning** is the second component of the Wealth Management Edge. It addresses the range of your important financial needs beyond investments in the four key areas described in Chapter 2: wealth enhancement, wealth transfer, wealth protection and charitable giving. As you've already seen, these noninvestment-related concerns are extremely important to your long-term financial success. Yet they are often overlooked or viewed (incorrectly) as secondary concerns. Therefore, very few investors address these four concerns in any systematic, comprehensive manner. For these reasons, the four main areas of advanced planning will be discussed in detail in Chapters 5 through 8.
- **Relationship management** is the third and final component. It involves fully understanding your critical needs and meeting those needs over time through a consultative process, assembling and

managing a network of financial specialists, and working effectively with any professional advisors you deem necessary (who may include financial advisors, attorneys and accountants). Relationship management is a key part of building and maintaining a successful wealth management plan, because it is what will enable you to maximize your success at both investment consulting and advanced planning. Relationship management will be reviewed more closely in Chapter 9.

Be aware that to realize these and other powerful benefits, you must bring true wealth management resources and capabilities to bear on your financial life. As you can see, the Wealth Management Edge approach is highly defined and consists of very specific steps.

You are your family's CEO

The Wealth Management Edge stands in stark contrast to how most of us operate today. Investors, even highly affluent ones, rarely take this type of co-ordinated and comprehensive approach with their finances. The vast majority tend to address financial needs and goals like retirement and estate planning on an ad hoc basis—treating these issues as separate concerns and placing each one in its own discrete "box." These investors fail to address the complex range of interconnected issues they face, and fail to do so in a coordinated manner.

This leads to challenges that can jeopardize the financial health of their families, their businesses and themselves. This is why the Wealth Management Edge is so important: It lets you see the big picture at all times and manage your finances around the whole instead of focusing on only one aspect.

Unfortunately, many financial advisors and other professionals also take an ad hoc approach instead of being comprehensive. They deal with issues only when they arise, and gather just enough information to implement one particular response to the current problem at hand. You may have noticed, for example, that many financial firms these days say that they offer wealth management. Typically, though, they focus almost exclusively on investment management. They may offer a few additional services, but they lack the truly comprehensive approach that you need to coordinate your entire financial life.

To truly make the Wealth Management Edge a part of your financial life, you need to recognize an important fact: You are the chief executive officer of your family. Being the CEO of your family (or the co-CEO, along with your spouse) means that you have a duty to define a vision for your family—what it is that you truly value and want to achieve together—and determine the best path to make that vision a reality (just as the CEO of a company must define the firm's direction and path).

Part of being a wise CEO of your family means deciding where you may want to get specialized help on your journey toward realizing your vision. The most common area where "family CEOs" look for guidance is in the area of finances, from someone who can act as a family's personal chief financial officer, or CFO. This is because, in many ways, the financial side of any family unit is a lot like the financial side of a business. In both cases, there are important decisions to be made about spending, saving, investing and planning for future growth. And as with any business, you and your family need a financial leader who can present you with good ideas, act as a sounding board and work with you to ensure that you have what you need to make smart decisions about your money—just as the CFO at a company would do.

Some CEOs of their families choose to also act as their families' CFOs—committing to thinking through the full range of financial challenges they face and developing optimal responses that work in concert with each other. Others choose to find a trusted financial professional, such as a wealth manager, who can act as their families' personal CFO and work with them collaboratively. This is a decision that you must make consciously and carefully, based on your ability and willingness to be a successful CFO of your family. But whether you act on your own or work in partnership with a professional financial advisor who uses the Wealth Management Edge, you will give yourself a tremendous advantage over other investors who take a more simplistic approach to managing their financial lives.

The Wealth Management Edge process

The Wealth Management Edge approach is arranged around a series of five meetings that work together to help identify key challenges and implement a range of ideal recommendations. The five meetings are:

1. The Discovery Meeting

The first step is to help you accurately uncover and clearly understand your true financial requirements—what you want and need most out of life. Without this knowledge, the most advanced investments in the world wouldn't do much good because they won't serve a larger purpose for investing. The Discovery Meeting therefore involves a systematic, detailed interview process that enables you to define your financial needs, goals and current position—giving you the information needed to create a comprehensive and accurate profile of yourself that will be used to create recommendations and work with other advisors who may be involved in the wealth management process. The overarching goal of this step is to understand your unique situation on a deep level—your key goals and values—and identify the challenges you face in achieving what is most important to you, so that the optimal plan can be designed. Because this part of the process is so critical to your success—and because few investors ever do a formal Discovery Meeting interview—we focus extra attention on this step below.

2. The Investment Plan Meeting

At this meeting, a detailed investment plan is presented (designed around the information uncovered during the Discovery Meeting) that describes your needs and risk tolerances and provides benchmarks for tracking progress toward your goals. The investment plan serves as the road map that will maximize the probability of growing and preserving your wealth over time. If you choose to act as your family's CFO, you will create this plan yourself. If you work with an appropriate wealth manager, he or she will present this plan.

A well-crafted investment plan will help ensure that rational analysis is the basis for your investment decisions, making you less likely to act on emotional responses to short-term or one-time events. Each investment plan should include these six important areas of discussion:

- Your long-term needs, objectives and values
- A definition of the level of risk that you are willing to accept
- The expected time horizon for your investments
- The rate-of-return objective and asset classes that will be used
- The investment methodology that will be used
- A strategic implementation plan

3. The Mutual Commitment Meeting

It's important that you consider the investment plan thoroughly before committing to work with a wealth manager acting as your personal CFO or moving forward on your own. At this meeting, which occurs after you have reviewed the plan carefully, you go over any questions or concerns you have about the plan to determine whether to move ahead and implement the recommended investment strategies. If so, the investment plan is put into motion.

4. The 45-Day Follow-up Meeting

This meeting is an opportunity to organize the various statements and paperwork that will have accumulated during the 45 days since you implemented your plan. It also allows a wealth manager to help you understand and organize the financial paperwork involved in working together (if applicable). It's also an opportunity to review any initial concerns and questions so that you understand exactly what the plan is for your assets.

5. Regular Progress Meetings

A wealth management plan must be regularly reviewed and updated as needed, and an advanced plan addressing your critical noninvestment goals must be designed and implemented as well. Regular Progress Meetings focus on reviewing the progress you've made toward meeting your various investment consulting and advanced planning goals and making any necessary adjustments based on relevant changes in your personal, professional and financial situation.

The Discovery Meeting and Total Investor Profile

One reason the Wealth Management Edge approach is so effective in addressing investors' needs is because of the Discovery Meeting. This initial stage of the process is focused on helping you identify your deepest, most important financial wants and needs.

The reason for starting with this meeting is simple: You cannot overcome the complex and sometimes conflicting challenges you face until you position your assets around the values, needs, goals and issues that are most important to you as a person and/or your family. Only then will you maximize the probability of your wealth supporting all of the things you want to accomplish.

The Discovery Meeting helps you identify all that is truly important to you in seven key areas of your life. If you choose to work with a financial advisor, there must be a close and thorough understanding between the two of you in these seven areas—a base of understanding that goes well beyond the simplistic and rudimentary aspects of a typical financial review. Your answers to the types of Discovery Meeting questions shown below will enable you to develop a holistic, all-encompassing picture of who you are and what you want from life, so that your assets can be positioned to support you appropriately:

1. **Values.** What is truly important to you about your money and your desire for success, and what are the key, deep-seated values underlying the decisions you make to attain them? When you think about your money, what concerns, needs or feelings come to mind?

2. **Goals.** What are you most proud of achieving in the past, and going forward, what do you want to achieve with your money over the long run—personally and professionally, from the most practical to your biggest dreams?

3. **Relationships.** Who are the most important people in your life—including family, employees, friends and even pets?

4. **Assets.** What do you own and with what liabilities—from your business to real estate to investment accounts and retirement plans—and where and how are your assets held?

5. **Advisors.** Whom do you rely on for advice, and how do you feel about the professional relationships you currently have? Is there a need to find new trusted professional advisors? Wealth management is designed to work in partnership with all of your trusted advisors to arrive at comprehensive recommendations that complement each other.

6. **Process.** How actively do you like to be involved in managing your financial life, and how do you prefer to work with your trusted advisors?

7. **Interests.** What are your passions in life when you are not working—including your hobbies, sports and leisure activities, charitable and philanthropic involvements, religious and spiritual proclivities, and children's schools and activities?

You (or a wealth manager) will then use your answers to these questions to create a Total Investor Profile that will serve as a road map—a guide so that every financial decision you make supports what you want most from life. (See **Exhibit 3.1.**)

If, like most affluent investors, you currently work with one or more financial advisors, you are probably aware that most use some type of fact-finding process when first meeting with clients or prospects. But have you ever noticed that these questions usually focus entirely on your assets and net worth? In contrast, note that only one of the seven categories that make up wealth management's Total Investor Profile concerns assets. Six of the seven are focused on helping you (and the wealth manager, if you use one) better understand who you are as a person so that you can make sure that any strategies or tactics you implement are aligned with who you are and what you want to achieve.

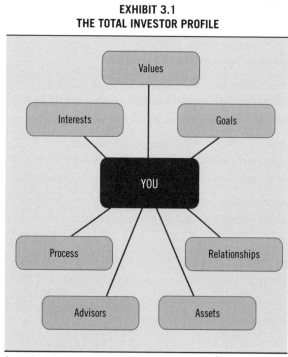

EXHIBIT 3.1
THE TOTAL INVESTOR PROFILE

Source: Prince & Associates and CEG Worldwide.

There's a big advantage to getting at this information. By engaging in this discovery process and using the insights learned from it to create a personalized profile, your wealth and all the choices you make about it become perfectly aligned with the life you want to build for yourself, your family and those you care about most.

The power of mind mapping

As you go through the Discovery Meeting, consider using a process called "mind mapping" to create a one-page graphic representation of your Total Investor Profile. When I coach financial advisors who use these mind maps, they tell me that their clients like seeing their financial situations presented in a graphical way.

Mind mapping will help you create a more useful profile for several reasons:

- It helps you to drill down to your key issues faster and more accurately.
- It captures information quickly yet in a highly organized format on one page.
- It makes it easy to link and cross-reference very different yet connected pieces of your financial picture.
- It helps you become more involved in the discovery process, motivating you to think about all the information you need to complete a comprehensive profile.
- It provides a basis for moving forward, with clear goals and next steps.
- It provides you with a document that is fast and easy to review.
- It is an excellent starting point for brainstorming ideas with other professional advisors you work with.

There are four elements to every mind map:

1. **The subject.** This is the center of attention and focus of the entire map—in your case, that means you and your family.
2. **Major themes.** These are major topics that radiate from the subject. These themes should correspond with the seven categories of the Total Investor Profile: values, goals, relationships, assets, advisors, process and interests.
3. **Branches.** These connect the subject and major themes with each other and with associated details.
4. **Structure.** The entire structure of the mind map is held together by the branches, forming an interconnected picture.

To create a Total Investor Profile using mind mapping, use an artist's pad or notepad. Write down your name in the center of the paper and circle it. Then begin the discovery process. If your first topic is your values, write "values" near your name, circle it and connect it back to your name with a line. As you uncover your most important values, write them down and connect them with one another as appropriate.

Exhibit 3.2 shows a sample of a Total Investor Profile that was created using mind mapping. As you can see, by the time you have completed the Discovery Meeting and created your mind map, you will have a one-page profile that has captured your most important issues, is packed with relevant detail and suggests the next steps you should take with your financial life.

The importance of values

Of the seven categories that make up the Total Investor Profile, the most important is the one representing your values. In fact, one of the most important conversations you can ever have with yourself, your family and your advisors is about your values.

Why are values so powerful? Because they are one of the core motivations for everything we do in our lives. They have a profound impact on every important decision we make, from what we choose to do for a living to whom we marry to how we spend our free time—in short, who we are as people. For example, you probably value your family above almost everything else in the world. As a result, you want to help them as much as you can. For many of us today—especially those who are part of the so-called sandwich generation—that might mean taking care of parents as they age, adult children as they leave the nest and build lives for themselves, and grandchildren as they grow up. Financially speaking, one of the things you might want to do is build an adequate college fund for a grandchild's education or set aside money to help an adult child start a business.

These are common goals among many affluent families today. But underlying these and similar goals is a fundamental value: loving your family. Values run the gamut from basic (such as security, financial freedom and not having to worry about paying the bills) to deep (such as family, community, faith and reasons for being.)

As important as values are, however, most of us are not particularly good at articulating them. We may act definitively on our values, but most of us have not necessarily thought deeply about exactly what those values are. The Discovery Meeting interview process can therefore bring substantial advantages to the process of managing wealth effectively. One of its primary purposes is to help you uncover your core values systematically and clarify them so you know where to focus your efforts.

One way to go about this is to ask yourself this question: "What is important to me about money?" Let's say that your first answer is "Security." You would then want to ask yourself, "Well, what is so important to me about security?" You might decide that the answer is "Knowing that I can take care of my family." You would then ask, "What is important to me about taking care of my family?" You would continue uncovering your values in this way until there is nothing more important to you than the last value you stated. At that point, you will have uncovered your single most important value.

EXHIBIT 3.2

TTHE TOTAL CLIENT PROFILE MIND MAP: A SAMPLE FAMILY

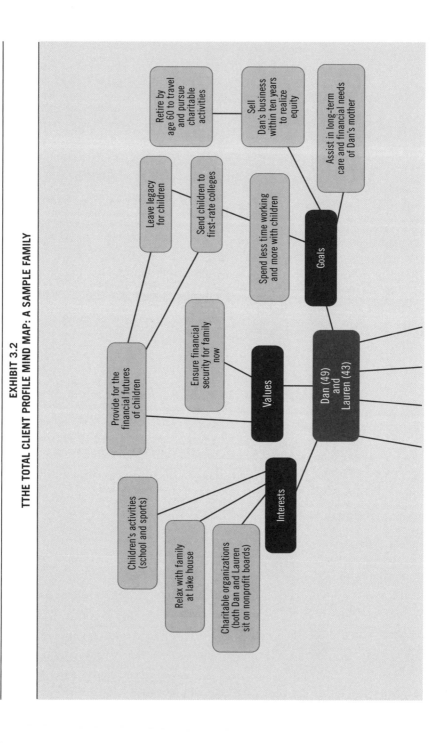

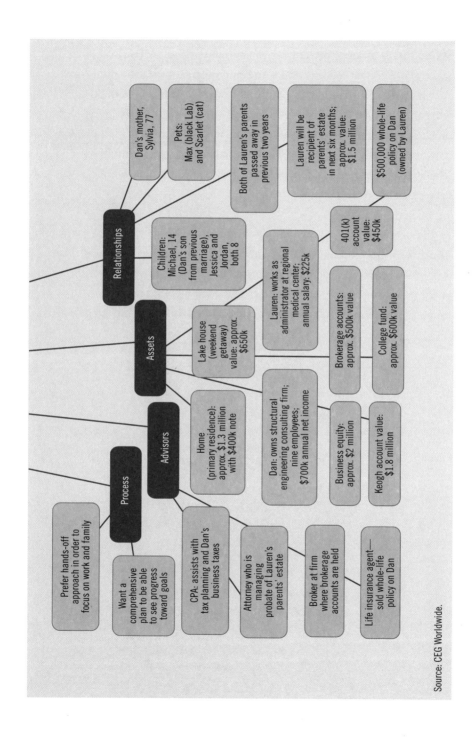

Relationships

Dan's mother, Sylvia, 77

Pets: Max (black Lab) and Scarlet (cat)

Both of Lauren's parents passed away in previous two years

Lauren will be recipient of parents' estate in next six months; approx. value: $1.5 million

$500,000 whole-life policy on Dan (owned by Lauren)

Children: Michael, 14 (Dan's son from previous marriage), Jessica and Jordan, both 8

Lauren: works as administrator at regional medical center; annual salary: $225k

401(k) account value: $450k

Assets

Lake house (weekend getaway) value: approx. $650k

Brokerage accounts: approx. $500k value

College fund: approx. $600k value

Advisors

Home (primary residence): approx. $1.3 million with $400k note

Dan: owns structural engineering consulting firm; nine employees; $700k annual net income

Business equity: approx. $2 million

Keogh account value: $1.8 million

Process

Prefer hands-off approach in order to focus on work and family

Want a comprehensive plan to be able to see progress toward goals

CPA: assists with tax planning and Dan's business taxes

Attorney who is managing probate of Lauren's parents' estate

Broker at firm where brokerage accounts are held

Life insurance agent— sold whole-life policy on Dan

Source: CEG Worldwide.

THE WEALTH MANAGEMENT EDGE APPROACH

While this is straightforward on the surface, it's important to realize that it takes perseverance to drill down to your most important value. Most of us simply don't spend a lot of time thinking consciously about the issue. That is why, although the values discovery process is something that investors can do on their own, most find that the best results occur by having a collaborative conversation about values with a financial advisor who employs the Wealth Management Edge approach and asks questions designed to uncover the core values that motivate them.

In the chapters that follow, you'll learn about each of the three main components of wealth management—investment consulting, advanced planning and relationship management—in more detail. Armed with this information, you'll be ready to bring the Wealth Management Edge to bear on all of your financial issues and maximize the probability of realizing your biggest goals.

Investment Consulting: Growing and Preserving Your Wealth

INVESTMENT CONSULTING:
GROWING AND PRESERVING YOUR WEALTH

IT'S TIME TO ADDRESS WHAT IS PROBABLY THE TOP FINANCIAL CON-
cern for most of you today: preserving your wealth. You have
worked hard for your money and you want to effectively grow and
preserve that wealth. Not primarily so that you can see that your wealth exists
on a monthly investment statement—although that can be reassuring—but so
that it can be there to help you meet your challenges and fulfill the many goals
that give your life meaning.

Remember that at the end of the day, you are the CEO of your "family enterprise." That means that, whether you do it all yourself or work with financial
professionals, you ultimately are the person responsible for making the decisions that will determine whether you will achieve your financial dreams. To
do so successfully, you need what every successful CEO has: a comprehensive
approach to addressing those issues.

To get started, take a minute to quickly review the Wealth Management Edge
approach from the last chapter, using the following formula:

> Wealth management (WM) = Investment consulting (IC) +
> Advanced planning (AP) + Relationship management (RM).

The first element of wealth management is investment consulting: the management of investments over time to help achieve your financial goals. It is
through the investment consulting process that you will address the primary
financial concern of wealth preservation.

Tune out the noise

Investment consulting is the core element of the Wealth Management Edge—
the foundation upon which you will build a comprehensive plan for managing
your entire financial life. Astute investment consulting requires you to deeply
understand your most important challenges and then design investment strategies that reflect your time horizons for various goals and tolerance for risk. It

also requires you to review your financial life on a regular basis so that you can make adjustments to the investment strategies as needed.

Not surprisingly, this is a tall order. These days you are inundated with information from every direction. As an investor who wants to make smart decisions about your portfolio, you know about the sheer volume of financial data and commentary bombarding you from the Internet, television, newspapers and magazines. It can be extremely difficult—seemingly impossible, even—to sift out what is genuinely useful and to leave the rest. It all begins to sound like noise.

Unfortunately, it's easy to get caught up in all that noise, because we are "wired wrong." Instead of using the information to make decisions thoughtfully and logically, we get drawn into the emotion generated by the noise. And when people begin to base their financial decisions on their emotions, I believe that they very often make mistakes. They chase hot stocks and market sectors while ignoring investments that are undervalued and poised to rise. They forget about risk and volatility. As a result, they often lose money and fail to preserve their wealth or they earn subpar returns that fail to help them achieve their financial goals.

To help you understand how emotion can lead you to make investing mistakes, let's look for a moment at what might happen when you hear about a stock.

If you are like many investors, you do not buy the stock right away. Remember, you are a sophisticated investor now because you have had the experience of losing money on an investment—an experience you did not enjoy—so you do not rush out and buy the stock immediately. Instead, you decide to follow it for a while to see where it goes. Sure enough, it starts to trend upward.

You follow the stock for a while as it rises. What's your emotion? Confidence. You hope that this might be the one investment that makes you a lot of money. You probably will do a little research on the Internet and even call a stock-broker. Let's assume that it continues its upward trend. A new emotion kicks in as you begin to believe that this just might be the one. This new emotion? Greed. You decide to buy the stock that day.

You already know what happens next. As soon as you buy the stock, it starts to drop. Everyone has had this experience. You are flooded with new emotions: fear and regret. You are afraid that you have made a terrible mistake. You no longer care about making a profit. You promise yourself that if the stock just goes back up to where you bought it, you will never do this again. You don't want to have to tell your spouse or significant other about it. You don't care about making money on the stock anymore; you just want out now.

Now let's say the stock continues to drop. Yet another emotion—panic—takes over. In your panicked state, you cannot help yourself: You sell the stock at a huge loss. And what happens next? New information comes out and the stock races to an all-time high. (See **Exhibit 4.1**.)

Emotions are powerful forces that sometimes cause you to do exactly the op-posite of what you should do—in this case, buying high and selling low. If you were to do that over a long period of time, you would cause serious dam-age not just to your portfolio but, more important, to realizing your financial goals. Remember from Chapter 2 that the average stock fund investor earned just 3.8 percent annually during the past 20 years, even though the S&P 500 gained 9.1 percent a year over that period.

The good news is that there is an alternative to noise-based investing. By applying a handful of sound investing concepts to your portfolio, you can tune out the noise and remove the emotion from your investment decisions. These success drivers will help empower you as you move toward achieving consistent long-term success in preserving your wealth. We turn to those concepts next.

EXHIBIT 4.1
THE EMOTIONAL CURVE OF INVESTING THAT HAPPENS ALL TOO OFTEN

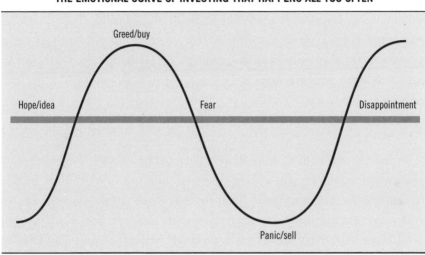

Source: CEG Worldwide.

Six success drivers for preserving your wealth

If you examine your own life, you may find that it is often the simpler things that consistently work in helping you to achieve your goals. Successful wealth preservation is no different. However, as we have just seen, it is easy to have your attention drawn to the wrong issues. These wrong issues—the noise—can derail your journey.

To keep on track, consider the following six success drivers as you make your decisions. Alone, each is a pearl of investing wisdom. Used together, they have the potential to maximize your ability to create and preserve wealth.

One: Create a road map

This particular success driver is hugely important, yet often underappreciated by investors. Only by knowing exactly where you are now and where you want to be in the future can you identify what you need to do to get there.

INVESTMENT CONSULTING: GROWING AND PRESERVING YOUR WEALTH

Start by assessing your current situation. Determine your net worth, your investable assets and any other financial resources you may have. Next, clearly define your investment goals. These could include college expenses for a grandchild, helping aging parents financially with health care or other costs, retirement, travel plans, a vacation home and so forth. Specify what you will need and when you will need it. By engaging in a Discovery Meeting and creating a Total Investor Profile as described in Chapter 3, you will be able to arrive at these answers quickly.

With these issues clarified, you will be ready to address the gap between where you are now and where you want to go. Determine how much of your income you can put toward your goals. Estimate the rate of return you will need to achieve on your investments to reach those goals. Consider how much risk you should take, and align your strategy accordingly. Select the investment vehicles you will employ, and then implement your plan.

This type of gap analysis often uncovers ways to better preserve your wealth. For example, one financial advisor whom I have worked with at our financial advisor coaching firm cites a client who works in the investment management business and earns a great deal of income each year. When the financial advisor first met him, he was taking on significant investment risk through his aggressive investment approach. A review of the investor's goals, net worth, and spending and saving habits revealed that he was taking on far more risk than was necessary. In fact, the financial advisor determined that this person could achieve all of his stated goals and retire comfortably by holding mainly municipal bonds and other lower-risk assets and targeting a 4 percent annual return. As a result, the financial advisor helped the client transition to a portfolio that incurred just as much risk as the client needed—but no more. When the market plummeted a few years ago, this client was extremely well-positioned and avoided the severe losses that he would have incurred if he hadn't worked with the financial advisor.

The key to creating a successful road map is to adopt an overall investment philosophy that you have confidence in and will stick with over time. For example, when developing an overall portfolio asset allocation strategy, you will want to consider which approach is the right fit for you. You may choose to take a strategic approach in which you set a target mix of stocks, bonds and other assets that will stay relatively consistent over time. Conversely, you might favor a tactical allocation stance, in which you shift your mix of assets regularly based on the outlook for those assets.

Likewise, when selecting investment vehicles for your portfolio, you will want to consider whether you favor an active management approach (in which you attempt to outperform the market's overall rate of return), a passive management approach (which focuses on attempting to deliver the return of specific market indices) or a combination of the two. And, of course, you'll need to determine the specific types of investment vehicles that best suit your plan and goals. As you're no doubt well aware, the options today are practically limitless—from traditional investments such as stocks, mutual funds and real estate to newer entries such as exchange-traded funds to alternative investments, including hedge funds and similar vehicles.

The specific details of these issues are beyond the scope of this book—indeed, all of the above subjects could be (and have been) the focus of their own books. The key point to remember is that the most successful affluent families take a well-thought-out approach to their investing and remain consistent in their methods over the long term.

This process of creating an investment road map may sound daunting and, depending on your situation, it can be. Many people, especially those families with more complex financial lives, find the assistance of a financial advisor acting as their personal CFO to be invaluable in creating their financial road maps and implementing their investment plans. In fact, closely examining your current situation and creating a detailed investment plan should be the first step that any financial advisor takes in working with you.

INVESTMENT CONSULTING: GROWING AND PRESERVING YOUR WEALTH

If you do choose to work with a financial advisor, consider a wealth manager who can assist you with your financial concerns beyond investments. In Chapter 9, we will look at what you should expect from a wealth manager so that you can make an informed decision when choosing which financial professional to work with.

Regardless of whether you create your road map yourself or consult with a financial advisor to create one, the road map will serve as a steady reminder of your goals and the clear-eyed decisions you have made to move toward your goals. Especially during times of market tumult when the emotions of others are running high, this will help you maintain your deliberate approach.

Two: Leverage diversification to reduce risk

Most people understand the basic concept of diversification: Don't put all your eggs in one basket. That's a very simplistic view of diversification, however. It can also get you caught in a dangerous trap—one that you may already have fallen into.

For example, some investors have a large part of their investment capital in their employers' stocks. Even though they understand that they are probably taking too much risk, they don't do anything about it. They justify holding the position because of the large capital gains tax they would have to pay if they sold, or they imagine that the stocks are just about ready to take off. Often, investors are so close to particular stocks that they develop a false sense of comfort.

Other investors believe that they have effectively diversified because they hold a number of different stocks. They do not realize that they are in for an emotional roller-coaster ride if these investments share similar risk factors by belonging to the same industry group or asset class. "Diversification" among many companies in the same industry is not diversification at all.

But truly diversified investors—those who invest across a number of different asset classes—can lower their risk and enhance their ability to achieve their goals. Because they recognize that it's impossible to know with certainty which asset classes will perform best in coming years, diversified investors take a balanced approach and stick with it despite volatility in the markets.

To illustrate this point, one financial advisor I have coached told me about a client who is a senior manager at a privately held firm. In 2006, he had more than 50 percent of his wealth invested in the firm's illiquid stock and stock options. On top of that, 90 percent of his portfolio of liquid assets was invested in stocks. Seeing this extreme lack of diversification, the financial advisor went to work—first creating financial models to assess the expected return and the risk of the illiquid stock and the options and then evaluating the portfolio of liquid assets.

The financial advisor and his client determined that by diversifying away from stocks and into fixed-income investments in the liquid portfolio, the client would maintain an extremely high probability of achieving his primary goal—retiring within the next ten years—while also significantly reducing the impact that bad returns from the stock market could have on his wealth. Even after taking into account the costs associated with selling out of his stocks—such as opportunity costs, taxes and transaction costs—the financial advisor and client agreed that diversifying was the wisest course of action.

The end result: The client's well-diversified portfolio sidestepped the worst losses during the market turmoil that began just two years later and performed much better than it would have if the client had continued to hold all that stock. More important, the client is still on track to achieve his retirement goals on time and as planned.

INVESTMENT CONSULTING:
GROWING AND PRESERVING YOUR WEALTH

Three: Seek lower volatility to enhance returns

If you have two investment portfolios with the same average or arithmetic return, the portfolio with less volatility will have a greater compound-rate-of-return potential. This means that you want to design your portfolio so that it has as little volatility as necessary to help you achieve your financial goals.

Why is this the case? Assume that you are considering two mutual funds. Both have had an average arithmetic rate of return of 8 percent over the past five years. How would you determine which fund has performed better? You would probably expect both to have the same ending wealth value.

However, this would be true only if the two funds have had the same degree of volatility. If one fund is more volatile than the other, the compound returns and ending values will be different. This illustrates the mathematical fact that the investment with less volatility will have a higher compound return potential.

EXHIBIT 4.2
LESS VOLATILITY = GREATER WEALTH

Year	Consistent Investment: $1,000,000		Volatile Investment: $1,000,000	
	Rate of Return	Ending Value	Rate of Return	Ending Value
1	8%	$1,080,000	30%	$1,300,000
2	8%	$1,166,400	-20%	$1,040,000
3	8%	$1,259,712	25%	$1,300,000
4	8%	$1,360,489	-20%	$1,040,000
5	8%	$1,469,328	25%	$1,300,000
Arithmetic annual return	8%		8%	
Compound annual return	8%		5.39%	

Source: CEG Worldwide. Note: This is a hypothetical series of returns to indicate the significance of volatility and does not represent any specific investments at any specific time.

You can see in **Exhibit 4.2** how this works. In this example, two equal investments have the same arithmetic rate of return but have very different ending values because of volatility.

As the CEO of your "family business," you should want the less volatile investment—not only because it helps you ride out the emotional curve, but because it may help you create the wealth you and your family need to reach your financial goals.

Four: Diversify globally to enhance returns and reduce risk

Investors in the United States tend to favor stocks and bonds of U.S.-based companies. For many, it's much more comfortable emotionally to invest in firms that they know and whose products they use than in companies located on other continents.

Unfortunately, these investors' emotions are causing them to miss out on a way to potentially increase their returns. That's because the U.S. financial market, while the largest in the world, represents less than half of the total investable capital market worldwide.[5] By looking to overseas investments, you could increase your opportunity to invest in global firms that can help you grow your wealth.

Global diversification in your portfolio has historically helped reduce overall risk. American equity markets and international markets do not always move together. In investing, there is a correlation between risk and return: Individual stocks of companies around the world with similar risk have the same expected rate of return. However, they do not necessarily get there in the same manner or at the same time. The price movements between international and U.S. asset classes are often dissimilar, so investing in both could help increase your portfolio's diversification.

---

[5]World Federation of Exchanges, *2010 Annual Report.*

INVESTMENT CONSULTING:
GROWING AND PRESERVING YOUR WEALTH

Exhibit 4.3 illustrates the potential benefits of diversifying your portfolio globally. Investors who focused solely on large-cap U.S. stocks, as represented by the S&P 500 index, would have lost money over the ten years from 2000 through 2009—a dismal decade, indeed. The story would have been far different, however, for investors who invested across a broad mix of different parts of the U.S. market as well as developed and emerging markets around the world.

EXHIBIT 4.3
TOTAL RETURNS OF VARIOUS ASSET CLASSES, 2000-2009

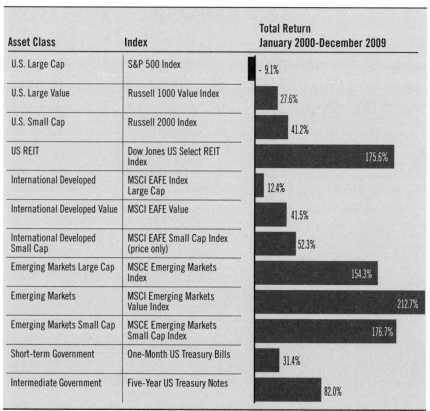

Asset Class	Index	Total Return January 2000-December 2009
U.S. Large Cap	S&P 500 Index	- 9.1%
U.S. Large Value	Russell 1000 Value Index	27.6%
U.S. Small Cap	Russell 2000 Index	41.2%
US REIT	Dow Jones US Select REIT Index	175.6%
International Developed	MSCI EAFE Index Large Cap	12.4%
International Developed Value	MSCI EAFE Value	41.5%
International Developed Small Cap	MSCI EAFE Small Cap Index (price only)	52.3%
Emerging Markets Large Cap	MSCE Emerging Markets Index	154.3%
Emerging Markets	MSCI Emerging Markets Value Index	212.7%
Emerging Markets Small Cap	MSCE Emerging Markets Small Cap Index	176.7%
Short-term Government	One-Month US Treasury Bills	31.4%
Intermediate Government	Five-Year US Treasury Notes	82.0%

The S&P data are provided by Standard & Poor's Index Services Group. Russell data copyright © Russell Investment Group 1995-2010, all rights reserved. MSCI data copyright MSCI 2010, all rights reserved. Dow Jones data (formerly Dow Jones Wilshire) provided by Dow Jones Indexes. Indexes are not available for direct investment. Index performance does not reflect the expenses associated with the management of an actual portfolio. Diversification neither guarantees a profit nor prevents a loss. Past performance is no guarantee of future results.

Five: Document your investment plan

One of the keys to success as an investor is to stay committed to your investment plan through thick and thin. But as you've seen, that is not always an easy task given the market's frequent volatility and the constant noise designed to distract you. For that reason, you will use an Investment Policy Statement, or IPS, to stay on track.

An Investment Policy Statement is a written document that spells out from top to bottom the ground rules for the most important aspects of your investment plan—from your overall investment philosophy and the investment goals you have identified to the specific investment vehicles with which you choose to implement your strategy.

The value of an IPS is that it can make you stop and ask yourself if a move you're thinking of making with your money is truly aligned with your best interests. By writing your personal investing "do's" and "don'ts" down on paper, you'll be perfectly clear not just about how you want to manage your investment capital over the long term, but also about the underlying reasons behind why you're investing as you are. This type of written reminder will provide important clarity and make it easier to maintain your investment plan and your disciplined approach in good markets (when you're tempted to load up on the hottest sectors) and bad (when short-term declines might prompt you to run for the exits).

Always remember: The key to success is to make smart decisions about your money consistently. An IPS can help ensure that consistency.

The particular makeup of your IPS will depend on your situation. However, to make sure the document adds value to your financial life, it should include the following components:

INVESTMENT CONSULTING:
GROWING AND PRESERVING YOUR WEALTH

1. Your long-term needs, objectives and values
2. Your risk tolerance
3. Your expected time horizon for your various goals
4. Your tax bracket and any other material information of your current situation
5. Your desired rate-of-return objective and the asset classes you will use in your portfolio
6. Your investment philosophy and methodology
7. Your parameters for reviewing and updating your plan

Six: Track your progress

As you move forward, assess your progress on a regular basis to determine whether you are still on track and whether you need to make any adjustments in response to changes in your personal situation or the markets.

Ideally, you will conduct this assessment on a regular basis. At a minimum, it should be done annually. If you choose to work with a financial advisor, he or she should facilitate a progress report each quarter.

To check your progress, you (or your financial advisor) should answer these questions:

- **Have there been any significant changes in your personal, professional or financial situation since the last progress report?** Do you expect any significant changes in the near term? Changes such as a retirement, divorce, birth of a child or grandchild, or death of a close family member can have a major impact on your goals and financial situation. This in turn can require adjustments to your investment plan.
- **How has the portfolio performed compared to the market?** Performance should be gauged against the benchmarks that represent the asset classes represented in your portfolio. So the performance of large-

company U.S. stocks or stock funds, for example, would typically be measured against the S&P 500 index.

- **Has the portfolio performance met its expected rate of return?** Your financial road map or investment plan should state the rate of return that is expected on your mix of investments. Compare this with the actual rate of return achieved by the portfolio.

- **What accounts for the portfolio's performance?** If your portfolio's performance is not matching your expectations or is falling below historical performance, find out why. It could be caused by short-term market fluctuations, or it could mean that your asset allocation should be adjusted.

- **Does the portfolio need to be rebalanced?** Portfolio rebalancing is designed to manage the risk you face as an investor. Rebalancing decisions are meant to help you continually buy low and sell high, by preventing you from being overexposed to overpriced assets and ensuring that you are not underexposed to attractively valued assets. Your decision to take either a strategic approach or a tactical approach to your portfolio will influence the method and timing of your rebalancing strategy.

- **What other changes, if any, should be made in the portfolio?** While we believe that a patient, long-term outlook is important to investing success, there are also instances where a change of course is indicated. Most often this will be in response to changes in your life or family, but it can also be called for by performance-related issues with particular investments.

By addressing each of these questions, your regular progress reports will become one of your most important tools for making disciplined, unemotional decisions about your investments.

Keep in mind that while these concepts are designed to maximize return relative to the level of risk you decide to take, no strategy can eliminate risk (which is inherent in all investments). Whenever you invest, you have to accept some risk. Also remember that as your family CEO you are ultimately responsible for reviewing your portfolio and risk tolerance and for keeping any financial advisors you work with current on any changes in either your risk tolerance or your life that might affect your investment objectives.

Investment consulting to achieve wealth preservation is just the first element of a comprehensive Wealth Management Edge plan. The next four chapters will focus on the key areas of advanced planning that you must address in order to effectively manage your entire financial life and achieve your goals: wealth enhancement, wealth transfer, wealth protection and charitable giving.

5

Advanced Planning Concern No. 1: Wealth Enhancement

"I see no new taxes, followed by some new taxes."

B Y ADDRESSING THE PRIMARY CONCERN OF WEALTH PRESERVATION through the investment consulting process, you will have built a solid financial base from which to move forward. The next step is to turn your attention to the key noninvestment concerns that you face. Remember that investments, while extremely important to your overall financial success, are just one component of the Wealth Management Edge process. To ensure that your entire financial life is truly "firing on all cylinders," you need to address the advanced planning issues that today's affluent investors share.

Take a moment to review the four areas of advanced planning:

1. **Wealth enhancement.** Your goal here is to minimize the tax impact on your financial picture while ensuring the cash flow you need.
2. **Wealth transfer.** This means finding and facilitating the most tax-efficient way to pass assets to your spouse, succeeding generations and any other heirs in ways that meet your wishes.
3. **Wealth protection.** This includes all concerns about protecting your wealth against catastrophic loss, potential creditors, litigants and identity thieves.
4. **Charitable giving.** This encompasses all issues related to fulfilling your charitable goals in the most impactful way possible.

Proactively enhancing wealth in an uncertain tax climate

To begin, let's examine the key issue of wealth enhancement. As Benjamin Franklin so famously noted, the only things that are certain in this life are death and taxes. There's not much any of us can do about overcoming death, of course. But taxes are a different story. There are plenty of ways to minimize your current, ongoing and future tax burdens in ways that are both technically feasible and legally sound.

Let's take a quick step back and set the stage for effectively thinking about and planning how to minimize taxes. First, you must recognize that the correct

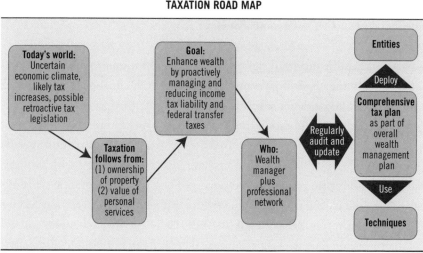

EXHIBIT 5.1
TAXATION ROAD MAP

Today's world: Uncertain economic climate, likely tax increases, possible retroactive tax legislation

Taxation follows from: (1) ownership of property (2) value of personal services

Goal: Enhance wealth by proactively managing and reducing income tax liability and federal transfer taxes

Who: Wealth manager plus professional network

Regularly audit and update

Entities

Deploy

Comprehensive tax plan as part of overall wealth management plan

Use

Techniques

Source: CEG Worldwide.

handling of taxes can have a big impact on your long-term wealth. Investors often consider tax issues only after they have fully thought through other investment and wealth issues. That's a big mistake. By legitimately minimizing your taxes through carefully proactive planning, you directly enhance your wealth and thereby further the achievement of all your other plans, goals, dreams and desires. The very nature of comprehensive wealth management demands that tax issues be given a prominent place through the entire wealth planning process.

As in the game of chess, one wrong tax move early on can lead to unwelcome or even disastrous results later on. Conversely, good tax planning can lead to huge tax savings both in the short term and in the long run. It therefore literally pays to take the time and make the effort to be sure that taxation issues are competently, effectively and proactively addressed.

Having a taxation road map can be enormously valuable. We will follow the road map set out in **Exhibit 5.1**. It starts with "Today's world," which is dominated by an uncertain economic climate. Unfortunately, not only do we have an uncertain economic climate, but we have uncertain tax laws and the real likelihood of substantial tax increases.

Tax laws are quite uncertain right now by reason of mounting pressure to increase taxes in the hope of relieving the problems of the national debt and continuing high budget deficits. It is important to note that everyone's tax situation is different. Our intention in this section is to raise awareness of potential issues, and you should consult with your tax advisor for information specific to your unique situation. It is clear, however, that wealth owners with substantial assets and income could be the targets of coming tax legislation. In addition, while the federal transfer taxes on gifts and estates have been changed for the better by the Tax Relief Act of 2010 (2010 TRA), these changes "sunset" (or disappear) on January 1, 2013, unless there is more legislation. Critically, if Congress fails to act by the end of 2012, the pre-2001 law comes back into effect automatically—with higher income, gift and estate tax rates and burdens.

Some more detail may be useful here for where we are at the time of the writing of this book. The federal transfer taxes (gift, estate and generation-skipping transfer, or GST, taxes) are intended to exact a levy on the transfer of wealth, whether that transfer happens by gift or through one's estate after death. The 2010 TRA provides, for 2011 and 2012 only, a 35 percent federal gift, estate and generation-skipping transfer tax rate, applied after a $5 million lifetime unified exemption per person. The $5 million is the highest exemption ever available, and many wealth owners should consider using it during their lifetimes with direct or trust gifts. Upon sunset of the 2010 TRA, much higher gift, estate and GST tax rates will come back into play, although hopefully more legislation will preserve these benefits. For many wealthy families, it will be important to take advantage of current tax laws while keeping reasonable controls over the assets transferred in trust.

Proactive planning requires ongoing attention to the legislative environment and a general understanding of the principles of taxation. While the U.S. tax code is complicated and detailed and generally defies understanding by those not trained in its intricacies, it can generally be said that taxation follows either (1) the ownership of property (capital) or (2) the value of personal services that are rendered.

Importantly, however, even the smartest investors and the best wealth managers are usually not specialists in taxation. For that reason, you or any wealth manager you work with will want to bring together a professional team that includes a tax specialist and a tax attorney. Because the Discovery Meeting process detailed in Chapter 3 has allowed you to delve deeply into everything from your goals and dreams to your risk tolerance, you (in partnership with your wealth manager, if you work with one) will be able to quickly and effectively communicate to these other professionals what it is that you feel is really important to you. The result will be a comprehensive tax plan that is part of your overall wealth management plan.

This comprehensive plan may make use of a variety of techniques—strategic and tactical proactive planning. It may also make use of a number of different entities, such as irrevocable trusts, corporations, family limited partnerships and family limited liability companies. Using the right techniques, and deploying the right entities, can make all the difference in terms of being successful in enhancing your wealth for the long run.

It's important, however, for neither you nor a wealth manager to simply assume that a finished tax plan will not need regular monitoring and updating. Instead, your team should regularly review the tax plan to make sure that it is being correctly implemented and to make sure that better options are not available.

Tax strategies and tactics to consider

When considering specific ways to proactively enhance your wealth in an uncertain and constantly changing tax climate, start with three big-picture concepts:

ADVANCED PLANNING CONCERN NO. 1: WEALTH ENHANCEMENT

1. **To enhance your wealth by minimizing unnecessary taxes, you must set yourself up to be successful on purpose.** Success does not happen on its own, especially when the rules of the game—in this case, the tax code and the way it has been interpreted by courts and the IRS—are created in such a way as to make the game difficult to play. Few laypeople are able to fully understand the tax code, much less take advantage of it. This means that you are likely to be far better off when you turn to a competent team of financial advisors for advice.

2. **The five major areas of financial concern cannot be seen in isolation.** It's essential to use an integrated, disciplined process for wealth management.

3. **As a wealthy individual, it's critically important to consider the best interests of younger-generation family members and any individuals who rely on your economic well-being.** A great deal rides on how well your wealth is managed, since it impacts not just you and your immediate family but everyone who is directly affected by your financial success and stability. You therefore want to develop specific goals and desirable scenarios and then test these goals and scenarios in terms of the personal, business and investment realities that hold true for you and all the members of your extended family.

Now let's turn to the tax strategies and tactics to explore. Keep in mind that the following information was accurate and relevant as of the writing of this book. However, before taking any action, you will want to consult with your tax professional to examine the options and determine the strategies that best meet your needs in the current tax environment

1. Take advantage of "opportunity shifting"

Taxation follows property ownership. If an "opportunity" exists—such as acquiring real estate at a low value or cheap stock in a startup company or embarking on a new and potentially highly profitable business—the early allocation of equity can shift substantial future asset values to a family's younger generations. And this can be done with the senior family members still in control as trustees, voting shareholders, partners or managing members in an LLC.

2. Make use of family-controlled entities

Entities are an important key to effective wealth management because they help ensure wealth preservation and asset protection even against the claims of creditors. Therefore, you might consider entities such as:

■ Irrevocable trusts of various types
■ C and S corporations
■ Family limited partnerships (FLPs)
■ Family limited liability companies (FLLCs)

These entities can generate significant and repeatable tax savings that can serve as a source of wealth enhancement. Consider the situation faced by one financial advisor's client, a 40-year-old self-employed consultant. During an annual review with his financial advisor, the consultant discovered that if he converted to an S corporation and paid himself a reasonable wage, he could potentially save up to $5,000 per year on taxes. John plans to work another 20 years. The future value of a $5,000 annual tax savings for 20 years based on a 10 percent-per-year investment return[6] is nearly $250,000. In short order, the consultant was able to improve his projected retirement wealth by close to a quarter of a million dollars.

Each type of entity has advantages and disadvantages, and an up-to-date analysis of your wealth should carefully consider the use of existing and potential new entities to ensure long-term and multigenerational wealth preservation. Not only do entities bear directly on the critically important issue of the ownership of capital, but they also clarify issues of management succession, often

---

[6]With the average compound rate of return for the Standard & Poor's 500 from January 1926 through December 2010 of 9.89 percent, I have used the time value of money of 10 percent for simplicity.

among the most difficult of family decisions. Since there have been proposals to restrict the uses of family-controlled entities, the wealth owner should act now to take advantage of the presently favorable tax laws.

3. Review life insurance opportunities

With ownership of life insurance policies by a trust or family member other than the insured, life insurance offers a number of ways to provide a tax-free or tax-deferred buildup of policy values. What's more, when life insurance policies are correctly implemented, they can provide a kind of "double tax-free benefit." This means that both deferred income tax benefits and estate tax reduction benefits result from having an appropriate family member or entity (someone other than the insured) be the owner and beneficiary of the policy.

4. Consider use of the intentionally defective grantor trust (IDGT)

One of the most income tax-friendly forms of trusts today is the "intentionally defective grantor trust" (IDGT), sales to which are treated as income tax neutral even when there is a completed transaction for gift and estate tax purposes. With the use of the IDGT, real estate that produces a net cash flow can be put into an irrevocable trust whose beneficiaries are next-generation members. The current-generation grantors pay any income taxes that arise, while the income is held in a tax-deferred irrevocable trust for the benefit of the children. This IDGT plan often is called the "gift that keeps on giving," because the trust assets build up without income tax liabilities.

5. Make loans to your children at low interest rates to buy valuable low-priced assets

Suppose that you loan your children $100,000 for nine years so they can buy valuable property or other assets. The IRS requires that you charge a minimum interest rate called the "AFR," or applicable federal rate, which was in the neighborhood of 2 percent for a nine-year loan as of July 2011 (there are also shorter- and longer-term loan rates). At the end of the nine years, after paying just the interest, the children are required to pay off the loan with a balloon payment. This structure can potentially benefit you in three ways. First, many assets, including income-producing property and family businesses, are still priced low because of the recession, limited capital and tight credit. Second, interest rates overall are low—the Fed has held them at historically low levels for quite some time—which means that the AFR is also low. And third, different types of "valuation discounts" are available and can be taken advantage of if, for example, less than a majority interest in a family business is sold.

6. Be aware of the importance of income tax basis

With the estate tax exemption at $5 million per decedent, there will be fewer taxable estates (at least in 2011 and 2012). In any event, the 2010 TRA restored for these two years (and likely thereafter) the "stepped-up" or increased income tax basis for appreciated property in a decedent's estate to fair market value. Wealth owners should ensure that there is complete tax basis information and data in their records and take basis into account when making gifts (which require a carryover basis) or sales within the family.

7. Review and take advantage of qualified retirement plans and IRAs

All tax-deferred retirement plans should be reviewed, including IRAs and Roth IRAs, to determine maximum investment potential and to adopt appropriate distribution strategies. Consider using a Roth IRA to avoid additional income tax on investment income. That's exactly what one financial advisor I work with did for a client recently. The self-employed client works in an industry where large swings in annual income are commonplace. After earning more than $1 million one year, he had negative income of $100,000 the next—a fact the financial advisor learned through his Discovery Meeting and Regular Progress Meetings with the client. Around this time, the client was seeking to invest in a private equity deal, which gave the financial advisor an idea: Convert some of the client's SEP IRA to a Roth IRA, move $100,000 from the SEP to the Roth (a tax-free transfer in this case because of the investor's negative income during the year) and invest in the private equity through the Roth. This strategy not only enabled a tax-free conversion, but also ensured that the client will never owe taxes on the (it is to be hoped, very large) gains from the private equity investment.

8. Watch out for passive losses

As a consequence of the IRS focus on leveraged passive investments, certain passive loss rules now are part of the Internal Revenue Code. Essentially, these rules prevent at least the total offset of passive losses against active income, such as executive compensation. Also, there generally must be objective and subjective economic substance present—substantial nontax reasons for the venture—before any losses can be recognized.

9. Consider the use of different types of trusts

A charitable remainder trust (CRT) can receive and then sell appreciated property, spreading the taxable gain from the sale over a number of years. Also, review the possibilities of various split-interest trusts, including the charitable lead trust (CLT) and the private trust known as the grantor retained annuity trust (GRAT). Note, though, that that the administration is once again proposing legislation that would be averse to the use of GRATs.

10. Turn personal expenses into legitimate business expenses

Consider the conversion of otherwise personal expenses into proper business or investment expenses that are deductible for income tax purposes. Also, review the opportunities in any family-controlled business or investment entities for younger-generation family members to "learn on the job," i.e., to be compensated as they develop valuable employment skills for the future.

Keep in mind that while you may be able to benefit greatly from these strategies, they are not enough in and of themselves to maximize your chances of achieving all that is important to you. They ultimately add up to one piece in the overall wealth management puzzle, albeit an important one. None of these five key areas of concern you face stands in isolation from the rest.

In the end, to set yourself up for success on purpose and be most effective, you need to deal with each area of your financial life systematically while maintaining an integrated approach to your overall financial picture. That integrated approach is what the Wealth Management Edge is all about. In the next chapter, you'll discover smart ways to transfer the wealth you have created to your spouse and younger generations in ways that are highly tax-efficient and that meet your needs and wishes.

6

Advanced Planning Concern No. 2: Wealth Transfer

"He inherited the throne, but that's all."

ADVANCED PLANNING CONCERN NO. 2: WEALTH TRANSFER

ESTATE PLANNING IS ONE OF THE MOST IMPORTANT YET MISUN-derstood areas of affluent investors' financial lives. While estate taxes often receive all the attention, they are only one relatively small element in the broader estate planning equation. You also need to focus on important issues such as management and wealth succession concerns, selection of successor managers or trustees, and preparing your heirs to successfully receive and make use of the assets they will eventually inherit.

To preserve, transfer and manage your family's wealth so that it lasts for multiple generations, you need to both understand the "big picture" and be up to date on the specific tactics that can make a difference to you right now. We will look at each in turn.

The big picture of estate planning: The 3 P's of people, property and process

It's useful to think of comprehensive estate planning in terms of three major categories, the "3 P's" of people, property and process.

People

The *People* category begins with you and your spouse. While one spouse is often financially dominant, either in terms of owning or creating more wealth or understanding more about finances, it is preferable for the non-dominant spouse to be treated as a fully equal partner in all conversations and decisions.

People also involves your children, grandchildren and other relatives. What do you want for them? What do they want for themselves? How involved are they in the process?

People may also involve identifying and working with a number of professionals and organizations, since the vast majority of investors—even highly sophisticated ones—lack the level of estate planning knowledge that is needed to create successful plans. A wealth manager who understands the structure and importance of estate planning may be the first professional you select. If so, it is important that he or she use the type of consultative process described in this book—one that is cooperative, communicative and proactive and combines goals with wealth issues to achieve multigenerational planning that supports both current goals and the family in the future.

This wealth manager should in turn work with a network of professional advisors (usually comprising at least an estate attorney, a high-end tax professional and a high-end insurance professional) as well as with any other financial professionals you work with to implement your integrated estate plan.

Finally, it may be appropriate to consider both the use of a trust company and the optimum jurisdictions for the trust company to be located in.

Property

Property includes wealth and assets of all kinds—money, investments, real property, personal property, retirement funds and potential inheritances—both presently and prospectively owned.

You may have what's called an "inchoate" interest, one that's not fully formed or real right now but that could turn into something very real and valuable in the future. If so, you certainly want to make its present value part of your calculations.

Similarly, you want to honestly evaluate the worth of all your current assets, including possible liabilities or changeable circumstances that might affect that wealth. For example, if a good deal of your family's wealth is tied up in a factory with a known asbestos or radon risk, then the cost of remediation, given current regulatory standards, must be realistically appraised and the value of the factory accordingly lowered.

ADVANCED PLANNING CONCERN NO. 2: WEALTH TRANSFER

Process

Process is the third part of the big picture. It refers to developing an estate plan to make optimum use of the legal entities (such as trusts), techniques and management initiatives that are most likely to effectively achieve your long-term wishes.

It's important to start the *Process* with an in-depth family history, making sure that the younger members of the family are part of this history taking and otherwise are fully engaged. The last element of the *Process* equation is often determining who will be responsible for executing the plan for the long run. This could be a family member or an individual trustee or a trust management company.

Estate planning tactics to explore

Estate planning has never been more important than it is right now, for two reasons.

First, we remain in a climate of low interest rates and depressed asset valuations, including valuations of family business assets. This makes a number of the tactics discussed below particularly relevant now.

Second, tax laws continue to be uncertain, especially with the political deadlock regarding the national debt and continuing deficits. Late in 2010, Congress and the administration enacted the Tax Relief Act of 2010 (2010 TRA). This act generally continued for two years—that is, 2011 and 2012—various Bush 2001 Act beneficial income tax provisions that had been set to expire. The 2010 TRA also re-enacted the federal estate tax back to January 2010 and provided quite beneficial estate and gift tax provisions for 2011 and 2012. Unfortunately, another crisis in tax law will occur on January 1, 2013. If there is no additional tax legislation by then, the estate and gift tax law will return to high 2001 levels. So acting now is important for wealth owners.

To tie things together, we categorize these top ten tactics according to the People, Property and Process framework. Given that the three categories overlap and impact each other, remember to keep the entire big picture in mind regardless of which particular tactics you consider.

1. Process: Review your existing estate plan

You probably have an estate plan, but often an in-depth review of the plan will show it to be out of date for various reasons. There may have been a change in marital status, for example, or the formula provisions of a will or living trust may no longer meet your goals, due to changes in the tax law. An outdated estate plan can expose you to significant risks. For example, one financial advisor I work with did a review of a client's will and found that it hadn't been updated for 15 years. As a result, the assumptions used in it regarding estate tax exemptions were completely inaccurate based on the current laws—meaning that he could potentially pay far more in estate taxes than he anticipated. What's more, the beneficiary designations on his IRA account (worth approximately $1.5 million) did not agree with the named recipients of the IRA in the will. As a result, the client faced the very real possibility that his assets would not go to the people he intended them to go to upon his death.

Unfortunately, there will likely always be some uncertainty about the estate tax law, which will require a regular review of estate planning documents on a systematic basis. This will ensure flexibility in your plan regardless of what Congress does or does not do. If you have not reviewed your estate plan in the last two years, you need to do it right now.

Also, the "succession planning" side of an estate plan requires constant evaluation of those persons or institutions named as successor managers or trustees. If you work with a wealth manager, he or she can provide input on trustee choices and include plan provisions that provide explicit guidance to successor managers.

ADVANCED PLANNING CONCERN NO. 2: WEALTH TRANSFER

2. Property: Create comprehensive financial statements

You need a personal, investment and business financial statement for your family, which you may want to develop in conjunction with a wealth manager and a CPA. This document should identify ownership and title for all assets, set forth realistic present values and projected future appreciation or depreciation in such values, and identify the current income tax basis for assets. Give careful attention to contingent liabilities, such as those associated with environmental hazards, contract disputes or litigation. It is also important to consider opportunities for acquiring new assets or businesses, since these can provide a sensible tax savings method that creates wealth for your family's younger generations.

This updated financial statement will provide you and your team of advisors with a strong foundation for developing your estate plan. This "financial snapshot" can also be used to develop a pro forma federal estate tax return that can help to identify those areas ripe for lifetime wealth transfers or other wealth shifting within your family.

3. People: Define your family goals

Once you have an understanding of the present state of your family's wealth, set short- and long-term goals. Each family has its own dynamics, and each generation within your family should be heard out and its views thoughtfully considered. Once an "inventory" of all family members is developed, then the senior family member (or members) can consider how to best match existing and future wealth with each family member.

Short-term goals to consider might include the directed education of younger family members, taking into account their wishes and expectations, so that they are capable of financial and business asset management. Choosing a successor manager among younger family members is an important option and must be considered in a manner that avoids conflicts within the family.

In the long-term goals area, the eventual distribution and protection of wealth down through the generations need to be analyzed and then documented as part of the overall plan. This is perhaps where institutional management is needed and where entities, including trusts with perpetual existence, can provide solutions to difficult challenges.

4. People: Consider alternatives for education funding

Carefully consider the various means available for funding the education of children and grandchildren. The tax law generally favors education of younger-generation family members, with a $13,000 per donor/per donee annual exclusion for gifts (periodically inflation adjusted) as of the date of publication, the unlimited gift tax exclusion for direct payments to educational providers and the availability of various tax-sensitive irrevocable trusts for children.

Also, in the event of your disability or death, your own will or revocable trust can include a special trust arrangement geared solely toward education. This type of trust can further include assistance for the young beneficiary in purchasing a home or starting a business, including appropriate provisions to ensure that the beneficiary is capable of handling such assets.

5. Process: Consider dynasty trusts

Irrevocable trusts are useful for protecting and managing your financial wealth, including equity positions in family-controlled business entities. Essentially, such trusts separate, as appropriate, the ownership of trust interests by beneficiaries from the management of the trust by the trustee(s).

So-called dynasty trusts, especially those located in states that have eliminated term limits on irrevocable trusts, can effectively control and manage financial assets for multiple generations. The gift and estate tax laws attach a penalty or extra transfer tax on transfers that skip one or more generations if the value of transferred assets is above certain limits. This is called the generation-skipping transfer, or GST, tax.

Therefore, effective tax planning usually limits generation-skipping transfers (that is, to grandchildren and lower generations) to the GST tax exemption ($5 million-plus in 2011 and 2012, but then back to close to only $1 million in 2013). Using the GST tax exemption is one of the more important planning considerations for 2011 and 2012 due to the uncertainty about 2013.

A dynasty trust allows for great flexibility in the distribution of income and principal over two or more generations. Therefore, a key decision to make at the outset will be your selection of the trustee or manager for such a trust. The trustee will usually have the ability to sell or purchase assets during the term of the trust, so changes in the asset mix of the trust can be made to address changed circumstances.

6. Property: Evaluate prospects for "opportunity shifting"

"Opportunity shifting" generally means the transfer of the power to acquire property before its actual acquisition or, alternatively, the transfer of property (such as startup company common stock) at its initial low value prior to any substantial increases in value. Since intrafamily transfers are taxed for gift and estate tax purposes at "fair market value" on the date of transfer, proper timing of such transfers is critically important. The rule of thumb is that one should sell or gift within the family at the lowest possible value but sell to a third-party outsider at the highest level of value.

You can use many techniques for opportunity shifting, including outright or trust gifts, cash loans to provide seed or option money to a family member, and deferred tax installment sales to a family member. Intrafamily transactions, including loans and sales, are required to bear interest. However, for both income and gift tax purposes, the tax law allows the interest rate used to be based on the currently quite low applicable federal rate for the term of the loan or sale. If a discounted asset—such as an interest in a partnership or limited liability company—is used in the sale, there is "double leverage" for the family shifting a wealth opportunity to the younger generation.

7. Process: Review your life insurance planning

Life insurance is generally considered a "wealth replacement" vehicle that adds to a family's wealth by counteracting IRS liabilities (such as estate tax liability), mortgage debt, or potential real estate and business liabilities. Life insurance is also often used as a funding vehicle for buy-sell agreements, where a key decision is whether the business entity or the individual equity owners should own the life insurance on an owner's life.

Since premiums paid for life insurance coverage are usually nondeductible for income tax purposes, an important goal should be to ensure that your life insurance is "double tax-free." This means that on maturity, the policy owner receives the proceeds without any income tax being due and also that such proceeds are not subject to any estate tax as part of the insured's estate. This result can be achieved even when the insurance policy has built up significant investment value in addition to the mortality coverage (death benefit) it provides.

However, to maximize the leverage of life insurance as a wealth replacement vehicle, the insured cannot be the policy owner—that is, cannot have any "incidents of ownership." A top financial advisor such as a wealth manager should be able to show you how an irrevocable life insurance trust can achieve this result without your losing control over the policy yet still ensure that the eventual proceeds received are used for their intended purposes.

Using the $5 million lifetime gift tax exemption currently in place could involve funding an irrevocable trust with investment assets, the income from which could be used to buy life insurance on the wealth owner's life. This can be done "double tax-free"—on the insured's death, the proceeds received by the trust would be both income- and estate-tax-free.

ADVANCED PLANNING CONCERN NO. 2: WEALTH TRANSFER

8. Process: Structure a favorable entity package

While trusts have many uses, an entity package with corporations (C or S), family limited partnerships (FLPs) or limited liability companies (LLCs) is often an effective way to (a) shift wealth opportunities within the family, (b) ensure management succession, and (c) save substantial gift and estate tax liabilities through valuation discounts for the transferred entity's equity interests. This area has seen a good deal of litigation over the years, and the IRS often audits family-controlled entities and transfers of entity interests. Taking action now is important, since adverse tax legislation could restrict valuation discounts using entities.

It's important that a qualified valuation appraiser is brought in as part of the planning team to consider the level of discounts. However, for entity planning to succeed, a real and significant nontax purpose for use of the corporation, FLP or LLC is required. Tax lawyers have developed "factors for success" in entity planning, as well as a "two step" valuation approach, which can allow you to substantially leverage your intrafamily gifts and sales without adverse tax consequences.

9. People: Determine your charitable goals and gifting alternatives

Over the years, many affluent families develop the goal of including substantial charitable giving in their estate plans. There are numerous options, from outright cash or securities gifts to charity to the use of highly specialized "split interest" gifts that have an element of family wealth shifting included.

For example, a designated account with a community foundation allows for a measure of your input as to the foundation's grants from your account while providing you with the maximum charitable deduction allowed by law. On the other hand, while private foundations are much more complicated and yield fewer charitable deductions, they can be effective ways of gifting a charity with an interest in a family business entity.

A wide variety of trusts can be used to implement charitable goals. These include the "split interest" trust technique, the charitable remainder trust, the charitable lead trust, the qualified personal residence trust and the grantor retained annuity trust.

10. Property: Prepare the family business for transfer or sale

As a family business enterprise matures, a common decision that needs to be made is whether to plan for keeping the business "all in the family" or to prepare the business for sale to an outside entity. (Becoming a public company and outright liquidation are also possibilities.)

Even where the family business will be sold or liquidated, act first on any desirable intrafamily transfers, because such transfers can usually be made at much lower values before any presale activity or negotiations take place. The business analysis here can be quite detailed, so your other advisors should be involved in the "sell or hold" decision-making process. Often certain investment assets within the family business need to be transferred out of the business entity prior to sale of the business itself. This raises planning opportunities and enables you to avoid tax pitfalls.

As you consider these strategies, keep in mind an important estate planning "don't." Although tax benefits are typically an extremely important issue in an affluent investor's estate planning process, you should never let taxes dictate your estate planning at the expense of other key considerations. If you allow taxes to drive your estate plan, you may experience unforeseen and potentially disastrous consequences.

One such situation involved a family that owned a vineyard. The vineyard assets were placed in an irrevocable trust in order to minimize the eventual estate taxes. That part of the plan worked well; after the father died, the family side-stepped a huge tax bill. But over time, the business was not nearly as successful as the family hoped, causing the matriarch of the family to want to sell some of the land that vineyard was on, in order to fund her expenses. However, the terms of the trust stated that she could not sell any of the land without the permission of her children—who refused to allow her to sell. As a result, her lifestyle was impacted significantly.

The upshot: Tax-related issues are a key part of an estate plan—but they are only one part and must be balanced with other needs and concerns.

Also remember that, as with all the areas of your financial life, estate planning and wealth transfer strategies must be revisited regularly to ensure that they still are appropriate for your situation and still make sense given your needs and goals as well as your concerns regarding your spouse and younger generations.

In the next chapter, we take a closer look at the third key advanced planning issue facing today's affluent investors: Protecting your wealth against major threats such as catastrophic loss, potential creditors, litigants and identity thieves.

7

Advanced Planning Concern No. 3: Wealth Protection

"Look, I'm not blaming you. I'm just suing you."

ADVANCED PLANNING CONCERN NO. 3: WEALTH PROTECTION

IN THIS CHAPTER, WE WILL ADDRESS THE THIRD CRITICAL ADVANCED planning concern: protecting your wealth. You have worked hard for what you have, and the last thing you want is to lose it through the carelessness, thievery or even maliciousness of others. By thoughtfully protecting it against catastrophic loss, potential creditors, litigants and identity thieves, you help ensure that you and your loved ones will be able to achieve your goals.

The four areas of wealth protection concern

In today's world, we are all concerned about protecting what we have—not just our financial assets, but our property; our confidential information; and, most important of all, our loved ones. "Wealth" includes everything that we hold near and dear.

To help organize your approach, it's useful to break down the specific protection concerns that the affluent share. For perspective, we turn to the most comprehensive wealth protection study I have ever seen—a national survey of 427 individuals, each with a minimum net worth of $1 million, that was conducted by our former director of research, Russ Alan Prince, and two industry experts, Paul Michael Viollis and Asa Bret Prince. Although the study was conducted in 2004, the results remain as relevant today as they did back then. They identified the following four broad security and protection concerns:

1. Protection concerns for self and loved ones

Not unexpectedly, the research found that those surveyed care most about the safety and well-being of themselves and those they hold most dear. As you can see in **Exhibit 7.1**, the top concern in this area is about a predator targeting loved ones, with 77.5 percent of those surveyed saying they were very or extremely concerned about this. This is followed by worry about a loved one being abducted (57.1 percent), acts of violence against a loved one (56.7 percent) and security for self when traveling internationally (49.4 percent).

EXHIBIT 7.1
PROTECTION CONCERNS: SELF AND LOVED ONES

Concern	Very or extremely concerned
Predators targeting a loved one	77.5%
A loved one being abducted	57.1%
Acts of violence against a loved one	56.7%
Security of self when traveling internationally	49.4%
Robbery or mugging of a loved one	35.4%
Predators targeting self	21.1%
Security of loved ones when traveling internationally	15.7%
Acts of violence against self	13.8%
Security of self when traveling domestically	12.6%
Security of loved ones when traveling domestically	11.5%
Robbery or mugging of self	8.4%
Personally being abducted	4.7%

N=427 wealthy individuals.
Source: Russ Alan Prince, Paul Michael Viollis and Asa Bret Prince, *Safe & Sound*, 2004, Natl. Underwriter Co.[7]

2. Protection concerns about confidential information

Given the prevalence of identity theft and the frequency with which secure databases are compromised, protecting confidential information is the second-most-important category of concern. We don't want others to have unauthorized access to our personal information.

Identity theft is the most prevalent concern in this area, cited by 77.5 percent of those surveyed. This is followed by access to private business information (42.6 percent), access to their or their loved ones' medical records (41.0 percent), and someone seeking to damage their personal or professional reputations (40.7 percent). (See **Exhibit 7.2**.)

---

[7]I chose to use this study even though it is somewhat dated because, to my knowledge, it is the most comprehensive study of wealth protection among the affluent and ultra-affluent ever done.

ADVANCED PLANNING CONCERN NO. 3: WEALTH PROTECTION

EXHIBIT 7.2
PROTECTION CONCERNS: CONFIDENTIAL INFORMATION

Concern	Very or extremely concerned
Identity theft	77.5%
Someone gaining access to private business information	42.6%
Someone gaining access to their or their loved ones' medical records	41.0%
Someone seeking to damage their personal or professional reputations	40.7%
Someone eavesdropping on them or their loved ones	26.9%
Extortion	8.0%

N=427 wealthy individuals.
Source: Russ Alan Prince, Paul Michael Viollis and Asa Bret Prince, *Safe & Sound.*

3. Protection concerns about financial assets

The vast majority of the affluent have worked hard for their wealth and therefore are quite concerned with protecting it. In this category, they are most worried that someone may take advantage of their progeny for financial gain, with 72.6 percent of those surveyed reporting this as a concern. (See **Exhibit 7.3.**) Whether they see their children or grandchildren as lacking financial sophistication or just real-world experience, they view offspring as a potential weak spot in their efforts to protect their wealth. Next in importance is concern about lawsuits from people they know, such as former spouses, ex-employees and former business associates (67.9 percent). Also of importance in this category is concern about being the target of lawsuits from people they do not know (58.5 percent), embezzlement in their companies (48.5 percent) and doing business with unscrupulous people (46.6 percent).

4. Protection concerns about property

The fourth category of concern is about property, with specific concerns about property ranking highest on the list. First is concern about their houses being burglarized (56.0 percent), followed closely by concern about vandalism to

---

EXHIBIT 7.3
PROTECTION CONCERNS: FINANCIAL ASSETS

Concern	Very or extremely concerned
Someone taking advantage of their children or grandchildren for financial gain	72.6%
Being targeted by unfounded or frivolous lawsuits by people they know	67.9%
Being targeted by unfounded or frivolous lawsuits by people they do not know	58.5%
Embezzlement at work	48.5%
Doing business with unscrupulous people	46.6%
Being the victim of financial fraud	10.1%
Hiring unscrupulous financial advisors	5.4%

N=427 wealthy individuals.
Source: Russ Alan Prince, Paul Michael Viollis and Asa Bret Prince, *Safe & Sound.*

EXHIBIT 7.4
PROTECTION CONCERNS: PROPERTY

Concern	Very or extremely concerned
Their houses being burglarized	56.0%
Vandalism to their houses	52.5%
Loss of valuables such as jewelry, artwork, pets, etc.	29.7%
Vandalism to other property such as cars, planes, yachts and artwork	26.9%
Transporting valuable property or documents	20.6%

N=427 wealthy individuals.
Source: Russ Alan Prince, Paul Michael Viollis and Asa Bret Prince, *Safe & Sound.*

their houses (52.5 percent). Next is concern about the loss of valuables such as jewelry, artwork and even pets, cited by 29.7 percent of those surveyed. (See **Exhibit 7.4.**)

As you review each of these four categories, think about your own level of concern in each. Which categories concern you the most, and which concern you the least—and do you have your priorities straight? How effectively do you think you are currently protecting yourself and your loved ones in each area?

Keeping these questions in mind, we will turn next to the specific ways that you can manage your risk in order to gain greater peace of mind.

Managing your risk

We do not live in a perfectly safe world. Risk is everywhere, and we cannot eliminate the threats to our wealth. The good news is that we certainly can take informed, measured steps to substantially reduce their *likelihood* and *potential impact.*

There are two ways you can protect your wealth. First, you can *mitigate risk.* This means taking actions that will minimize your exposure to a risk and, should that risk occur, reduce its impact. As you will see, there are many ways to mitigate risk, depending on the situation.

Second, you can *transfer risk*, or shift it away from yourself and to another party. The most common means to transfer risk—though certainly not the only way—is to purchase insurance.

What follows is a brief overview of the primary ways in which you can mitigate and transfer risk in each of the four areas of wealth protection concern identified earlier. Because every situation is unique, no single set of recommendations is right for everyone. However, you should be aware of the range of options so that you can begin to make decisions about what you need, what you can implement on your own and what you may need assistance in implementing.

Protecting yourself and loved ones

Managing risk in this area is focused on safeguarding yourself and your loved ones from harm, in particular from violence and abduction.

Mitigate the risk:

- **Create a crisis contingency plan.** Security training conducted by professionals can often reduce the risks of being involved in a crisis situation. Having a contingency plan in place, should a crisis occur, will help ensure a timely, more-effective response.
- **Conduct background checks.** Very often the weak link in personal security is someone on the "inside"—an employee or contractor of the family or business. For this reason, it's wise to conduct thorough background assessments both at the time of hire and periodically thereafter.

Transfer the risk:

- **Obtain appropriate insurance.** Kidnap and ransom insurance covers losses due to kidnapping, extortion, detention or hijacking for items such as ransom reimbursement, loss of income and medical care. Policies can also provide for the services of a crisis management team.

Protecting your confidential information

Here, your main concern is defending your private information from those who would use it for financial gain and, in the process, hurt your own financial standing and reputation.

Mitigate the risk:

- **Protect your personal information.** Never provide your Social Security number unless absolutely necessary. Do not carry your Social Security card, passport or birth certificate with you unless there is a specific reason. Keep photocopies of your credit cards in a safe place. Carry only the cards you will need. Never provide personal information to anyone in response to an unsolicited request, including emails.

- **Protect your documents.** Shred all unneeded documents containing personal information. Secure personal information in your home, especially if you employ outside help. Do not leave your mail in the mailbox overnight or leave outgoing mail in your mailbox for pickup. Better yet, get a locking mailbox.

- **Protect your communications.** Guard your computers with up-to-date virus- and spyware-protection software. Do not use easily available information, such as your mother's maiden name, for the passwords for your online accounts. Password-protect the wireless connection at your home, and ensure that your cordless phones are digital.

- **Monitor your credit reports and financial statements.** Scrutinize both for any unusual activity. You may order one credit report per year from each of the three major credit reporting companies for free at www.annualcreditreport.com. Consider signing up with an identity theft protection service, which will monitor the use of your personal information and alert you when something is amiss.

- **React swiftly when a problem occurs.** If you do become the victim of identity theft, you should place fraud alerts on your credit reports, close accounts that have been tampered with and file a report with your local police. For details on these and additional steps you can take to resolve the specific problems caused by the theft of your identity, go to the Federal Trade Commission Web site at www.ftc.gov/idtheft.

Transfer the risk:

- **Obtain the proper insurance.** It may be beneficial to buy identity theft insurance, which will cover you for the costs associated with recovering your financial identity. This insurance is often made available as part of the package of services offered by identity theft protection services. It is also often included in homeowners or renters insurance or through credit cards or as a stand-alone policy. If you are already covered, determine whether the coverage is adequate.

Protecting your financial assets

In this area, your goals are to shield your assets from creditors, litigants and others who seek to unjustly take your wealth as well as to ensure that you have sufficient resources to cover your liabilities.

Mitigate the risk:

- **Conduct background checks on financial professionals.** Make sure that any wealth manager or other type of financial advisor that you are entrusting your money to is indeed trustworthy. An excellent starting point is the Financial Industry Regulatory Authority (FINRA), which offers a free online tool for researching the professional backgrounds of current and former FINRA-registered brokerage firms and financial advisors. It is available at www.finra.org/Investors/ToolsCalculators/BrokerCheck/index.htm.
- **Investigate potential business partners.** As with financial professionals, it's prudent to make sure you know the professional history of anyone you may be going into business with.
- **Get second opinions on major financial transactions.** Even when you are dealing with credible people, you should still determine whether they are making intelligent financial recommendations. Before making any large financial transaction, get a second opinion from a trusted tax advisor, attorney or other appropriate professional.
- **Leverage asset-protection strategies.** There are a number of strategies that can be used to protect assets from possible future liabilities. These are just a few examples:

  ❖ Specific forms of business ownership, such as LLCs
  ❖ Asset protection trusts

ADVANCED PLANNING CONCERN NO. 3: WEALTH PROTECTION

❖ Premarital and postmarital agreements
❖ Funded buy-sell agreements
❖ Use of state exemptions
❖ Gifting of assets

One example of a simple yet often overlooked asset-protection strategy is a declaration of homestead. Filing this declaration protects the value of a home from creditors' claims, lawsuits and bankruptcy. One financial advisor I have worked with helped a client implement this strategy and protected his home up to $500,000.

Asset-protection strategies are complicated, and some (including the declaration of homestead noted above) vary from state to state. It is crucial to work with a top attorney who can recommend the most appropriate strategies for you and then implement them ethically and effectively.

Transfer the risk:

■ **Verify that your life insurance is adequate.** If you do not have sufficient assets to fund all your liabilities (and potential liabilities, should you pass away), life insurance is one way to protect your wealth. It can be a complicated product, however, so work with an insurance specialist who focuses on the high end.

■ **Consider umbrella coverage.** One important yet often overlooked area is umbrella (or excess liability) coverage, which addresses your liability for lawsuits, medical bills and attorney fees if you injure someone or someone is injured on your property. This can be an especially important type of insurance for affluent families. One financial advisor we work with cites the example of a client worth $25 million who had no umbrella policy. If that client severely hurt or killed someone in a car accident, for example, his wealth could be wiped out in almost no time due to medical and lawyer fees. Even if someone slipped and fell during a visit to his home, he could find that his assets would be taken. With that in mind, the financial advisor helped the client find a $5 million umbrella policy that added a vital layer of protection to his assets and his overall financial security for less than a thousand dollars annually.

■ **Verify that your health and disability insurance is adequate.** These two types of insurance protect one of your most important assets—your earning power. The health insurance marketplace in particular is undergoing significant change, so work with a specialist who can obtain the best rates for the coverage you need.

■ **Consider long-term care insurance.** This type of insurance may not be right for you if you have adequate assets to self-insure for long-term care. Either way, it pays to examine the issue and make an informed decision.

■ **Monitor your Social Security account.** Social Security is one cornerstone of financial security, so check your annual benefit statements for accuracy to ensure that you get the full benefit to which you are entitled.

Protecting your property

In this final area, you are concerned about guarding not just the physical security of your home, but also the financial security of your property and business interests.

Mitigate the risk:

■ **Design and implement a comprehensive security system.** A well-secured property has robust systems in place for every part of the property. These are just some of the possible components:

❖ Perimeter security elements, including gates; fences; lighting; alarm system; camera system; access control system; and detailed access protocols for family, guests and staff

❖ Interior security elements, including alarm system, video surveillance, safes, interior lighting, access controls, emergency first aid and fire equipment, and safe rooms

❖ Security personnel, employed either by you or by a security firm

Transfer the risk:

■ **Assess your personal insurance coverage.** To make certain that you have ample coverage, work with a high-end insurance specialist. The reason: As you accumulate wealth, the mass market insurance options that used to suffice are often no longer adequate. Review your coverage in each of these applicable areas:

❖ Homeowners insurance

❖ Automobile insurance

❖ Art, jewelry and other collectibles insurance

❖ Personal excess umbrella insurance

❖ Watercraft insurance

❖ Aircraft insurance

■ **Assess your commercial insurance coverage.** If you have commercial interests, you should also review your coverage in key areas, including these:

❖ Business insurance, including commercial property and premises liability

❖ Directors and officers liabilities

❖ Professional liability

❖ Employee practices liability

The protection-planning process

As we have just seen, the list of potential protection ideas is long and many of those options are quite complex. And, as we said, no single set of recommendations is right for everyone. For these reasons, we urge you (or the professionals you work with) to conduct a methodical protection-planning process that includes these steps:[8]

1. Assess your risks.
2. Evaluate possible strategies.
3. Select the most appropriate strategies.
4. Create an action plan to enact protection measures.
5. Implement the measures according to the plan.
6. Follow up periodically to ensure that your changing needs are met over time with the latest technology and strategies.

You may recognize that your wealth protection concerns are serious and complex enough to warrant the services of specialists. If you work with a wealth manager, he or she should have these professionals in his or her network:

- An attorney who can design and implement astute asset-protection strategies
- A high-end insurance specialist who can make optimal insurance recommendations
- A security consultant with deep technical knowledge and experience addressing the protection concerns of people like you

Working together as a team and in close consultation with you, these professionals can create and implement a plan that will make sure that you and everything that is important to you are better-protected than ever before.

---

[8]Russ Alan Prince, Paul Michael Viollis and Asa Bret Prince, *Safe & Sound.*

8

Advanced Planning Concern No. 4: Charitable Giving

"Your legitimacy as a philanthropist is at stake."

ADVANCED PLANNING CONCERN NO. 4: CHARITABLE GIVING

THE FOURTH AND FINAL AREA OF ADVANCED PLANNING THAT we will discuss is charitable giving—using your wealth to make the greatest possible impact on the charitable causes you care most about.

Charitable giving has long been an area of importance for affluent individuals and families, of course. Interest in philanthropy has risen in recent years, fueled in part by two of the world's richest men: Warren Buffett, who has pledged to donate 99 percent of his fortune, and Bill Gates, whose Bill and Melinda Gates Foundation has become the largest private foundation in the world. Most recently, Buffett and Gates joined forces and asked a group of billionaires to commit to giving at least half of their wealth to charity.

You may not have billions. But if you are like many Americans, you are looking to use your wealth to benefit not just your family but also the world around you.

Giving away, getting back

To make wise decisions about your charitable giving, it's useful to start with an understanding of philanthropy today. How much are others giving? Where are they giving? What are their motivations? With this perspective in mind, you will be ready to undertake a thoughtful process that will focus and maximize your own giving.

In 2010, total charitable giving in the United States amounted to $291 billion. The great majority of this amount—81 percent—was individual giving and charitable bequests. The remaining 19 percent was giving by foundations and corporations. Despite the recent recession, total individual giving averaged $1,814 per household.[9] For affluent households, the number was no doubt significantly higher.

---

[9]*Giving USA 2011: The Annual Report on Philanthropy for the Year 2010* by The Center on Philanthropy at Indiana University. Published by Giving USA Foundation.

Where is all this money going? According to research, these are the top five types of recipient organizations:

1. Religious organizations (received 35 percent of all charitable donations in 2010)
2. Educational institutions and organizations (14 percent)
3. Grant-making foundations (11 percent)
4. Human services groups (9 percent)
5. Health organizations (8 percent)

Rounding out the list of major recipients of charitable giving were public-society benefit organizations (such as The United Way and donor-advised funds); the arts, culture and humanities; international affairs organizations; and environmental/animal organizations.

You can't say yes to all the causes that interest you or all the charitable requests you receive, so you need to decide what motivates you most to give. A study of high-net-worth households found that the top motivations behind their charitable behavior are:[10]

1. Believing that their gifts can make a difference (cited by 72.4 percent of those surveyed)
2. Feeling financially secure (71.2 percent)
3. Knowing an organization is efficient in its use of donations (71.0 percent)
4. Funding the same organizations each year (65.9 percent)
5. Giving back to the community (64.1 percent)

Other important motivators include political and philosophical beliefs, volunteering at a particular organization, and giving spontaneously to support a need.

---

[10] *The 2010 Study of High-Net-Worth Philanthropy* by The Center on Philanthropy at Indiana University.

ADVANCED PLANNING CONCERN NO. 4: CHARITABLE GIVING

The charitable planning process

Regardless of the reasons you have for making charitable giving a part of your financial life, you want to make the most of each dollar you give. Proper planning can help you maximize your philanthropic impact in a number of ways:

- **Leverage financial benefits.** You can ensure that your gift is fully leveraged to maximize its value to you and to the charitable organization.
- **Fully support your values.** Through your careful choice of charitable organizations and gift-giving vehicles, your giving is more likely to thoughtfully support your values.
- **Focus and streamline your giving.** When you have determined how much you want to give and when you should give it, it is easier to say no when you receive a request that is outside your plan.
- **Involve family.** Planning can create opportunities to involve family members and convey philanthropic values to younger generations.
- **Maximize tax benefits.** And last, but certainly not insignificant, careful planning helps ensure that your giving maximizes the tax benefits available to you.

As you formulate your charitable plan, we recommend that you take the following steps:

Step 1. Formulate your goals

When your giving reflects your deepest values and interests, philanthropy becomes powerful and profoundly rewarding. Consider these questions as you begin to create a charitable plan:

- **What do you care about most?** What causes are most important to you? What truly moves you—to laughter or to tears? What fascinates you, holding your interest over time and challenging you to always learn more?

- **What values do you want to convey with your giving?** Do you want to give back to the community, honor an individual, promote social justice, help sustain your church, support arts and culture, or focus your efforts on another area?
- **What do you hope to achieve with your giving?** How do you want the world to look different as a result of your philanthropy? Perhaps it will mean that a devastating disease has been eradicated, that qualified students will have the assistance they need to attend your alma mater, or that low-income families in your city will have safe and affordable housing.
- **Where do you want to make your impact?** What is your geographic focus? Is it on a local, regional, national or international level?
- **How involved do you want to be?** Some people prefer to simply give anonymously, while others want to be deeply involved in the organizations to which they give.

Step 2. Decide where to give

With your charitable goals defined, the next step is to identify the optimal charitable organizations for helping you achieve your goals. You may decide to deepen an existing relationship with a charity, or you may find that your best route is to identify other organizations.

To begin your search, ask people who are active in the causes that interest you for recommendations and talk to friends and colleagues who share your charitable interests about the organizations they support. On the Internet, several Web sites are very useful for both locating organizations that support your goals and for evaluating them to ensure that they are well-run and fiscally sound:

- Charity Navigator (www.charitynavigator.org)
- Better Business Bureau Wise Giving Alliance (www.bbb.org/us/charity)
- GuideStar (www.guidestar.org)

ADVANCED PLANNING CONCERN NO. 4: CHARITABLE GIVING

Once you have a list of candidates, confirm by looking at the mission statement of each that they support your goals. Each mission statement should clearly articulate the purpose of the organization and whom it serves. Next, verify that the programs are fully aligned with the mission. The mission statement and program information should be easily available on the organization's Web site. If not, contact the organization directly.

With your list narrowed to the most likely candidates, conduct further research to verify that they will use your contributions effectively and efficiently. Ask to review each organization's audited financial statements and IRS Form 990, which most public charities are required to file. This form provides information on revenue, expenses, key personnel and board members, as well as other information that will provide insight into how well the organization is being run.

If your contributions will be sizable and long-term, ask to conduct a site visit. The organization's executive director or a member of the executive team should be more than willing to meet with you to discuss the organization in depth, to introduce you to key personnel and to put you in touch with board members.

Step 3. Decide when to give

Next consider the timing of your gifts. Typically, individuals make contributions in three ways:

1. **Annual giving.** Regular, ongoing contributions are usually tied to the tax year to ensure that you receive maximum tax benefits. Planned annual giving benefits the recipient organizations because it allows them to better predict cash flow and plan for the future.
2. **Legacy giving.** Making philanthropy part of your legacy can extend your impact well beyond your lifetime. Legacy giving may involve a simple will bequest or more complex vehicles that allow significant assets to be transferred while the donor is still living.

3. **Giving in response to a crisis.** Many people are moved to give when disasters occur, and certainly these contributions can be helpful. But also consider a strategic approach, such as helping specific disaster-response organizations to build their infrastructures and expand their capabilities.

Depending on your goals and resources, you may choose to give in one, two or all three of these ways.

Step 4. Decide what to give

Finally, look at exactly which assets you are willing to invest in your charitable goals. These are the primary types of contributions:

- **Cash.** Donations are tax-deductible. Deductions may be subject to a portion of adjusted gross income, but the limits are quite high.
- **Appreciated stock.** This is also tax-deductible at full market value (if held for at least one year), but again there are limits—though high ones—on the deduction that may be made. Appreciated stock that is donated is not subject to capital gains taxes. This approach can be a good option for charitably inclined investors with low-basis stock holdings. Example: One financial advisor we coached started working with a client who had been selling stocks she had held for decades, paying significant capital gains taxes on the profits, and then writing checks to her charities with the remaining money. To maximize her giving, she began to donate appreciated stock directly to the charities instead of selling the shares first. It's estimated that this approach will save the client—who donates approximately $100,000 annually— around $15,000 in capital gains taxes each year that can be donated to the charities instead of sent to Uncle Sam.
- **Tangible property.** Virtually any type of property—from clothing to automobiles and real estate—can be donated. Tax deductions are again allowed, with certain limits.

- **Time and expertise.** While expenses related to volunteering are deductible, the value of your time is not.

Once you have moved through each of these four steps of the planning process, you will be well-equipped to make smart decisions about the specific vehicles you will use to optimize your giving.

Strategies and tactics for giving to consider

Your philanthropic goals and financial situation are completely unique to you. This means that no single way of giving is optimal for everyone. The following descriptions of the top ten giving tactics will give you a good overview of the key options available. Keep in mind, however, that the complexity of your charitable giving is likely to increase along with your wealth and the complexity of your overall financial life.

1. Checkbook philanthropy

These are gifts made in response to requests or one-time situations such as fundraising events. Such giving usually occurs with little advance planning by the donor and typically is not part of a strategic approach. As a result, it may not convey the maximum benefit to either the donor or the charitable organization.

2. Volunteering

This could involve volunteering to assist with an organization's program activities, serving on the board, helping with fundraising, providing pro bono professional services or otherwise becoming involved in its mission. In addition to being personally rewarding, volunteering gives you an insider's look at the needs and effectiveness of an organization.

3. Will bequest

This is a simple and easy type of planned charitable gift that allows you to benefit your charitable causes while enabling you to retain use and ownership of your assets while you are still alive. You can leave cash or property to a charity by including a bequest in your will or trust. For property that passes via a beneficiary designation (such as individual retirement accounts), you can designate the charity as beneficiary. The amount you give will not be subject to estate tax.

4. Community foundations

Community foundations are nonprofit organizations that pool the support of many donors to benefit a specified community. They are governed by boards of private citizens charged with speaking for the needs and well-being of the communities served. They generally offer a number of options for charitable giving, including donor-advised funds and donations to the foundation's unrestricted funds. The foundation invests and administers these funds, simplifying your charitable giving.

5. Donor-advised funds

Donor-advised funds are charitable giving accounts offered by sponsoring organizations, typically community foundations and financial services companies. They allow you to make contributions and receive immediate tax deductions, at the same time making recommendations for distributing the funds to charitable organizations of your choice on your own timetable. By aggregating donors and donations, donor-advised funds are able to keep administrative costs relatively low, and thus they offer an attractive alternative to private foundations.

ADVANCED PLANNING CONCERN NO. 4: CHARITABLE GIVING

6. Private foundations

Private foundations—often family foundations—are tax-exempt, nonprofit entities that make grants to charitable organizations. Typically established through a significant initial gift, they allow the founder full control over management of the funds and granting to charities. Foundations are overseen by boards, often comprising family members, friends and financial advisors, that make all major decisions about the direction of the foundation. In contrast to donor-advised funds, private foundations can have significant startup and legal costs as well as higher ongoing management costs.

7. Life insurance

Life insurance can be used to make charitable gifts in a number of ways, each one accomplishing slightly different goals and carrying different tax implications. These are several of the more common methods:

- The charity is named as beneficiary of the policy. The policy's proceeds will be passed free of gift and estate taxes.
- The policy owner gives an existing policy to a charitable organization. The donor may take an income tax deduction for the fair market value of the policy and deduct future premiums.
- Policy dividends are given to the charity. The value of the dividends is tax-deductible.

8. Charitable gift annuities

A charitable gift annuity is a contract between a charitable organization and a donor whereby the donor makes a gift to the charity in return for guaranteed fixed payments for the lifetime(s) of one or two individuals. The annuity payments are based on a set schedule: the older the age of the person (or persons) receiving the annuity, the higher the rate.

Most types of assets can typically be donated, including cash, securities, real estate, art and collectibles. Depending on the life expectancy of the donor and the anticipated income stream, there may be a partial tax deduction for the gift itself. A portion of each gift annuity is tax-free, with the remainder taxed at regular income tax rates. After the death of the last beneficiary, the remaining value of the annuity contract is distributed to the charity.

9. Charitable remainder trusts

A charitable remainder trust (CRT) is an irrevocable trust that receives cash or property from a donor, generates a potential income stream for the donor or his or her beneficiaries for life or a term of years, and then distributes the remainder to one or more charities selected by the donor.

A key advantage of CRTs is that they are tax-exempt. This means that the donor can contribute highly appreciated assets that the CRT can then sell without paying capital gains tax. The trustee may then reinvest the proceeds into a more diversified or higher-yielding portfolio. In addition, the donor may receive a partial income tax deduction based on the value of the eventual gift to charity.

There are two types of CRTs:

- A charitable remainder annuity trust pays a fixed dollar amount each year.
- A charitable remainder unitrust pays an amount equal to a percentage of the trust value at the beginning of each year.

10. Charitable lead trusts

A charitable lead trust (CLT) is the mirror image of a charitable remainder trust. It receives cash or property from a donor and generates an income stream from which it makes payments to a charity for a specified period. At the end of that period, it distributes the trust property to a specified beneficiary, usually family. Unlike CRTs, CLTs are taxable trusts, with income in excess of charitable deductions subject to tax.

Giving to charitable causes need not be overly complicated when you choose one or more of the straightforward giving vehicles. However, if you want to give substantial amounts and make the biggest possible impact for both the charity and your own financial situation, use of one or more of the more-complex vehicles may be appropriate. In this case, working with a professional financial advisor who in turn works with specialists in charitable giving can be extremely helpful in ensuring that your charitable dollars create the maximum impact you are looking to achieve.

By now, you may be thinking that addressing all the financial concerns you face—and doing so in a coordinated manner—is a significant challenge. Well, you're right. Building and maintaining an effective Wealth Management Edge plan takes a combination of effort and deep knowledge. That is why the vast majority of affluent investors enlist one or more professionals to help them design, implement, review and maintain their Wealth Management Edge plans. In the next chapter, you will see how to build and manage the right team of professionals who can help you maximize your ability to reach the financial goals you have set out for yourself, your family and your community.

9 Relationship Management: Your Team of Specialists

"I hereby empower you, Ambrose T. Wilkins, to water my plants. And let's hear no more talk about how I never delegate authority."

RELATIONSHIP MANAGEMENT: YOUR TEAM OF SPECIALISTS

A S YOU HAVE SEEN, SUCCESSFULLY MANAGING YOUR FINANCIAL life means not only identifying the strategies that will help you address your most important challenges but also implementing those strategies effectively. This brings us to the third and final element of the Wealth Management Edge approach: relationship management.

Remember that the Wealth Management Edge consists of three parts:

Wealth management (WM) = Investment consulting (IC) +
Advanced planning (AP) + Relationship management (RM).

Relationship management is all about getting the help that will allow you to do a great job at successfully managing your entire financial life over time. It means meeting your critical financial needs by building, managing and working with a network of professional advisors who have deep knowledge across the range of specialties that you require. As you will see, these professionals may include wealth managers, attorneys, accountants and others, depending on your situation.

Why relationship management matters

The reasons for building a team of specialists who can help you are obvious. For one, many of the tasks that you need to accomplish to build and maintain a strong financial future for yourself and your family—such as creating estate plans and implementing strategies to minimize taxes without incurring IRS scrutiny—are complex and time-consuming. Therefore, these tasks demand a high level of knowledge and focus.

The second reason is that no one can be a true specialist in all of the investment and advanced planning approaches that today's affluent families require. Think about all of the issues and strategies involved in each the five key areas of investments, wealth enhancement, wealth protection, wealth transfer and charitable giving. It is simply unrealistic to expect one person to have the knowledge and skills needed to successfully navigate all five of those areas. But by surrounding yourself with a group of specialists, you can ensure that you benefit from the best advice possible in each area.

This is true even among the very best financial advisors working today. Instead of trying to do everything themselves, top financial advisors go out of their way to build and manage professional networks on an ongoing basis. Why do they do this? So that they can bring the very best recommendations to their clients, of course. If you choose to work with a financial advisor, it is important to select one who has a network of professional advisors capable of providing the advice you need.

That said, working with the right team of professionals is a key step you must take regardless of whether or not you work with a financial advisor. Even the biggest "do it yourselfers" need to find and work with specialists from time to time. For example, few of us have the time, training or temperament to act as our own accountants, attorneys, business brokers and so on.

In short, it doesn't matter who you are: You will need to build relationships with professionals and manage those relationships on an ongoing basis if you want to be a successful CEO of your family.

Building a team of specialists

Let's assume that you choose to create your own team of financial professionals. You will need to take responsibility for the following actions:

- Building and managing the team on an ongoing basis
- Providing the team members with a deep understanding of your situation, goals and needs
- Holding regular meetings with the team members to draw out the optimal recommendations for you and your family

RELATIONSHIP MANAGEMENT: YOUR TEAM OF SPECIALISTS

So who should be part of your team of specialists? The most effective professional networks typically are made up of three core team members: a private client lawyer, an accountant and a life insurance specialist. These are the key professionals that you will work with regularly to address your advanced financial challenges and take advantage of financial opportunities.

Specialist No. 1: The private client lawyer

The private client lawyer is the key member of the team in virtually all instances. That is because he or she can address many of the tax, estate planning and legal needs detailed in the previous chapters—all critical areas of concern for solving the challenges you and your family face. You can expect a typical private client lawyer to provide the following services:

- Estate planning
- Wealth protection planning
- Income tax planning
- Succession planning
- Business planning for successful entrepreneurs
- Development of charitable giving programs
- Probate services
- Guardianship and conservatorship services

A lawyer who can provide these types of services can obviously bring tremendous value to an investor's life. Consider the example of a private practice physician who works with a financial advisor whom I have coached. This physician loves his work but doesn't have time for or interest in the day-to-day management of the business. And although the doctor was already very successful, the financial advisor suspected that he could be even more profitable with not much additional effort. The financial advisor therefore called in the attorney on his team of financial professionals, who proceeded to gather key benchmarking data for clinics of similar sizes to the doctor's—such as average bill per patient, average collection rates, number of employees, total payroll and revenue per employee. Armed with this information, the physician is now able to quickly evaluate and monitor the health of his business and make adjustments as needed to enhance his success even further.

Specialist No. 2: The accountant

While a private client lawyer will provide a big-picture perspective on tax planning, an accountant typically will have much more detailed, day-to-day knowledge of your income taxes. He or she should be able to make specific recommendations to mitigate these taxes.

Specialist No. 3: The life insurance professional

A good life insurance specialist will work closely with your private client lawyer to identify and structure a plan that leverages the entire range of life insurance options, such as those that have been discussed throughout this book.

Other specialists to consider

Beyond the members described above, there is a wide range of other professionals that you may need only occasionally—or perhaps just once.

For example, many affluent investors find that one of the first professionals they need to add beyond the core team is a personal lines insurance specialist—a property-casualty agent who works at the very high end of the market. These professionals can be so important in some cases that some affluent investors make them part of their core teams. In addition, you may need a credit specialist to evaluate your current loan situation. Other specialists that you may need on a one-off basis include a derivatives specialist who deals with concentrated stock positions; a securities lawyer who supports the work of the derivatives specialist; an actuary, who is often needed when dealing with certain life insurance issues; and a valuation specialist, who may be required to appraise your business interests, real estate or collectibles.

RELATIONSHIP MANAGEMENT: YOUR TEAM OF SPECIALISTS

Keep in mind that this list is only the beginning. Depending on your unique requirements, you may need to bring in other types of financial professionals to address highly specific challenges.

If you are building your own team from scratch, you will need to identify good candidates in these areas. Your best sources for finding potential specialists for your team are most likely your friends and associates—other like-minded people you know well and trust and who have goals and needs similar to yours. In addition, the specialists you work with may have professional networks of their own that they can refer you to.

The wealth manager option

An alternative to building your own team of professional advisors is to work with a wealth manager who can provide you with access to the resources you need and who can build and manage the team on your behalf. You often can tap into an entire team of specialists by essentially making one choice—which wealth manager to work with.

For example, wealth managers who use the Wealth Management Edge process described in this book focus primarily on helping investors with wealth preservation needs through investment consulting. They develop strong relationships with private client lawyers, accountants, insurance specialists and others and work with those professionals regularly to meet their clients' advanced planning needs.

Exhibit 9.1 illustrates a sample professional network that a good wealth manager will have in place. As you can see, the wealth manager's primary relationships are with the three core specialists: the private client lawyer, the accountant and the life insurance professional. These team members may have relationships with the other types of specialists that clients may need from time to time. The wealth manager's primary role is to be the general manager of this team—the one person who coordinates all their efforts on behalf of clients.

EXHIBIT 9.1
A SAMPLE PROFESSIONAL NETWORK

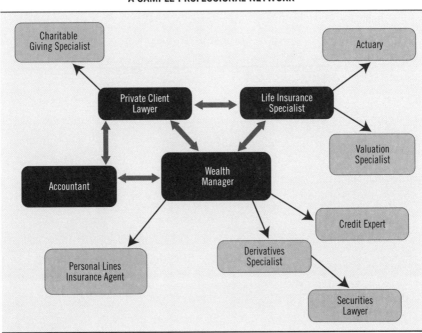

Source: CEG Worldwide.

Finding a top wealth manager

If you choose to work with a wealth manager for help with investments and advanced planning issues, look closely for evidence that potential candidates display the six traits that financial industry research[11] tells us most contribute to clients' satisfaction with their financial advisors.

I call them the 6 C's:

1. **Character.** Without doubt, any wealth manager you work with should have integrity, be trustworthy and be dependable. He or she

---

[11]Russ Alan Prince and David A. Geracioti, *Cultivating the Middle-Class Millionaire.*

should demonstrate these character traits in every contact with you and should exhibit self-discipline.

2. **Chemistry.** This is the wealth manager's ability to "connect" with you. You should feel a genuine rapport with him or her from your very first meeting. You should feel that the person understands who you really are—that he or she "gets you," essentially.

3. **Caring.** The wealth manager must have empathy for you as a person and should understand what is most critical to you, beginning with your life goals and financial objectives. Your wealth manager should care more about you than he or she does about making money.

4. **Competence.** Of course, the wealth manager should be smart and able to manage the technical aspects of your finances. Even better, he or she will be recognized as a leading professional in your area.

5. **Cost-effective.** This is not a question of what the wealth manager costs but one of whether he or she provides you with a high value for the relative cost.

6. **Consultative.** This is the most important factor because it frames your entire relationship with the wealth manager as an ongoing, long-term partnership. It has three major components:

   - **Cooperative orientation.** Some financial advisors feel it is their job to constantly hold their clients' hands and take care of everything for them. However, most clients actually prefer a more collaborative approach where they take an active part in the management of their finances. Wealth managers recognize this fact.

   - **Contact.** The wealth manager should ask you how often you would like to be contacted, how you prefer to be contacted and on what topics you want to be contacted. As appropriate, he or she should also reach out to you on matters beyond your finances.

■ **Customized communications.** The wealth manager should tailor his or her communications to you and your specific needs and interests. They should be sophisticated and highly professional—not off-the-shelf spiels.

As you choose a wealth manager—or take a closer look at your current financial advisor—keep in mind that you need someone to not just help you manage your investments, but also help you reach all of your most important financial goals. This is one of the most important financial decisions you will make, and you deserve to be extremely satisfied with your choice.

If you opt to work without a wealth manager, you will need to go out and find the various specialists mentioned above and then coordinate their efforts with your own. Remember that your core team should consist of a private client lawyer, an accountant and an insurance professional. To determine their suitability for your team, you can evaluate each professional on the same six characteristics mentioned above.

The professional network meeting

Once you have a team of financial professionals in place—either through working with the right wealth manager or through your own efforts—your various planning needs can start being met in a coordinated manner.

The setting for doing so is called the professional network meeting, which should be held at least once a year. The key objectives for each of these meetings: to identify, prioritize and document all opportunities for assisting you in each area of your financial life. The following section details how top wealth managers conduct their meetings with their teams. If you build your own team, you should consider emulating these steps to ensure maximum success.

RELATIONSHIP MANAGEMENT: YOUR TEAM OF SPECIALISTS

Step 1. Open the meeting

Take a moment to welcome everyone to the meeting. If there are any professionals present who are new to the network, briefly introduce them to the group and ask them to say a few things about themselves.

Step 2. Follow up on any open issues

If there are any open items that were discussed at previous meetings, follow up on them now. Keep this brief and high level. If you have detailed items involving one professional, avoid bogging down the entire team with your discussion. Instead, schedule a separate one-on-one meeting with that professional.

Step 3. Present your current situation

Take five minutes to present your Total Investor Profile (from Chapter 3). Be aware that network members, especially new ones, may ask for additional details and financial documents. If they do, remind them that this is a strategic, high-level conversation and that all you are asking for at this point is help on determining next steps.

Step 4. Facilitate brainstorming on the case

On a flip chart or whiteboard, draw out the framework for the advanced plan mind map, with your name in the middle connected to the four areas of advanced planning. Now ask your network members the first question: What can be done to help you with wealth enhancement and tax mitigation? Start with one professional, get his or her ideas, and then move around the circle until you have captured all ideas. There will likely be some jumping around as you do this; that's fine as long as you keep the conversation focused on the key question and capture all ideas. In brainstorming, you are looking for quantity over quality, so don't worry at this point about which ideas are best.

Once you have gathered all wealth enhancement action ideas, move on to the next advanced planning area of wealth transfer by asking this: What can be done to help you with wealth transfer? Write down ideas as you did before, and then move on to the two remaining advanced planning areas: wealth protection and charitable giving.

Once you have gathered all ideas for the four advanced planning areas, prioritize them by asking your team this question: What would we recommend that I do first? Your goal is to determine which actions should be taken first in order to make the greatest possible positive impact on achieving your key objectives.

Step 5. Take the next steps

Once you have finished, summarize the next steps. If you are running the meeting with your own professional team members, determine which action or actions should be taken and communicate that to the team. If the meeting is being run by your wealth manager, he or she will explain that the ideas generated at the meeting will be used to create an advanced plan that will be presented to you at your next meeting together.

Step 6. Close the meeting

Sincerely and enthusiastically thank the professionals for their involvement in your network and your financial life. Ask them for feedback on what did and did not work well and any suggestions that might make future meetings go even better. Finally, schedule the next meeting.

As you can see, working with the right team of specialists is a crucial part of the Wealth Management Edge process. A network of specialists adds value not only by identifying opportunities to improve your financial situation, but also by working with you or your wealth manager to implement and maintain the best strategies for capturing those opportunities.

RELATIONSHIP MANAGEMENT: YOUR TEAM OF SPECIALISTS

While some affluent investors choose to take the time to build, manage and regularly meet with their own hand-picked team of specialists, most prefer to tap into these teams through their relationships with wealth managers who have already created ongoing relationships with various specialists that their clients need.

Regardless of which approach you take, you will maximize your ability to achieve a highly successful financial life for you and your family if you get the help you need to achieve all that is important to you.

10 Putting It All Together

"What are your plans? Are you always going to be like this?"

PUTTING IT ALL TOGETHER

Y OU HAVE NOW LEARNED THE LESSONS AND STRATEGIES THAT some of the most successful families today use to make smart choices about their wealth—and you're ready to move forward by bringing the Wealth Management Edge to bear on your own financial life.

To help you do that, take a moment to review the key steps in the Wealth Management Edge process that will enable you to achieve the life you truly want for yourself and your family.

Step 1. Develop your Total Investor Profile

As you saw in Chapter 2, the vast majority of today's affluent families are concerned with five main areas when it comes to managing their financial lives: preserving wealth, enhancing wealth, transferring wealth, protecting wealth and donating wealth. To be successful in all of these areas (and any others of importance to you), you need to coordinate all the moving parts of your financial life so that they work together as effectively as possible.

The Wealth Management Edge accomplishes this in three ways:

1. Using a consultative process to gain a detailed understanding of your deepest values and goals and your most important financial wants and needs
2. Using customized recommendations designed to fit your unique needs and goals beyond simply investments
3. Implementing these customized recommendations in close consultation with your professional advisors

Remember from Chapter 3 that the Wealth Management Edge consists of three main components:

Wealth management (WM) = Investment consulting (IC) +
Advanced planning (AP) + Relationship management (RM).

■ **Investment consulting** is the foundation upon which any comprehensive Wealth Management Edge plan is created. It means positioning your investments around your goals, return objectives, time horizons and risk tolerance in order to preserve and grow your wealth.

■ **Advanced planning** is the second component of the Wealth Management Edge approach. It addresses the range of your important financial needs beyond investments.

■ **Relationship management** involves fully understanding and meeting your financial needs over time through a consultative process, assembling and managing a network of specialists, and working effectively with any professional advisors you deem necessary.

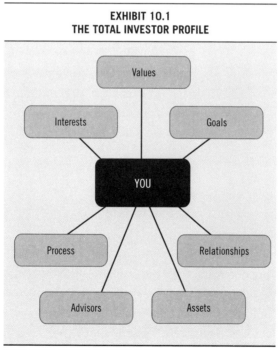

EXHIBIT 10.1
THE TOTAL INVESTOR PROFILE

Source: Prince & Associates and CEG Worldwide.

The best way to identify the specific issues, concerns and goals in your own life is to use the Discovery Meeting process described in Chapter 3 to develop a Total Investor Profile for yourself. (See **Exhibit 10.1.**) Remember that the Discovery Meeting helps you identify all that is truly important to you in the seven key areas shown below—thus enabling you to develop a holistic, all-encompassing picture of who you are and what you want from life, so that your assets can be positioned to support you appropriately.

Step 2. Create an investment plan

Once you have developed a Total Investor Profile, you can begin to address what is almost certainly the primary issue you face: growing and preserving your wealth.

To do so, you will implement the investment consulting component of the Wealth Management Edge process, which is designed to manage your investments over time to help achieve your financial goals. Astute investment consulting requires you to design investment strategies that reflect your time horizons for various goals and tolerance for risk. It also requires you to review your financial life on a regular basis so that you can take adjustments to the investment strategies as needed.

As seen in Chapter 4, there are six investment consulting success drivers that will help you grow and preserve your wealth:

- **Create a road map.** Start by examining your current situation—your net worth, your investable assets and any other financial resources you may have—as well as your investment goals. Then you will be ready to address the gap between where you are now and where you want to go. Determine how much of your income you can put toward your goals. Estimate the rate of return you will need to achieve on your investments to reach those goals. Consider how much risk you are willing to take, and align your investment strategy accordingly.

■ **Leverage diversification to reduce risk.** Truly diversified investors are those who invest across a number of different asset classes—various types of investments with their own distinct risk and reward characteristics. Effective diversification can lower overall risk, without necessarily sacrificing return. Because they recognize that it is impossible to know with certainty which asset classes will perform best in any given year, diversified investors take a balanced approach and stick with it despite volatility in the markets.

■ **Seek lower volatility to enhance returns.** You want to design your portfolio so that it has as little volatility as necessary to help you achieve your financial goals. The reason: If you have two investment portfolios with the same average (or arithmetic) return, the portfolio with less volatility will have a greater compound-rate-of-return potential. In short, you will generate more wealth through the less volatile portfolio—thereby increasing the probability of achieving your financial goals and preserving your wealth.

■ **Diversify globally to enhance returns and reduce risk.** Foreign investments are one of the best ways to potentially increase portfolio returns, because the U.S. financial market represents less than half of the total investable capital market worldwide. By looking to overseas investments, you could increase your opportunity to invest in global firms that can help you grow your wealth. What's more, the price movements between international and U.S. asset classes are often dissimilar, so investing in both could help increase your portfolio's diversification and reduce overall risk.

■ **Document your plan.** Use an Investment Policy Statement, or IPS, to stay committed to your plan. An IPS is a written document that spells out the ground rules for the most important aspects of your investment plan. By writing your personal investing "do's" and "don'ts" down on paper, you'll be perfectly clear not just about how you want to manage your investment capital over the long term, but also about the underlying reasons behind why you're investing as you are. This type of written reminder will provide important clarity and make it easier to maintain your investment plan and your disciplined approach in both good markets and bad.

■ **Track your progress.** As you move forward, assess your progress on a regular basis to determine whether you are still on track and whether you need to make any adjustments to your plan. The assessment should determine if there have been any significant changes in your life or family situation, how your portfolio has performed relative to the market and to its expected rate of return, the reasons behind your portfolio's performance, and whether you need to rebalance your portfolio's allocation to various asset classes.

Step 3. Prepare an advanced plan

Remember that investments, while extremely important to your overall financial success, are just one component of the Wealth Management Edge process. Once you have addressed your investment consulting needs, the next step is to turn your attention to the key noninvestment concerns that you face.

To ensure that your entire financial life is truly "firing on all cylinders," you need to address the four advanced planning issues that today's affluent investors share:

1. Wealth enhancement

Minimizing the tax impact on your financial picture while ensuring the cash flow you need.

Remember the following key concepts when considering specific ways to proactively enhance your wealth in an uncertain and constantly changing tax climate:

- **You must set yourself up to be successful on purpose.** Success does not happen on its own, especially when the rules of the game—in this case, the tax code and the way it has been interpreted by courts and the IRS—are created in such a way as to make the game difficult to play.
- **The five major areas of financial concern cannot be seen in isolation.** It's essential to use an integrated, disciplined process for wealth management.
- **Consider the best interests of younger-generation family members and any individuals who rely on your economic well-being.** A great deal rides on how well your wealth is managed, since it impacts not just you and your immediate family but everyone who is directly affected by your financial success and stability.

A comprehensive wealth enhancement plan may make use of a variety of techniques—strategic and tactical proactive planning. It may also make use of a number of different entities, such as irrevocable trusts, corporations, family limited partnerships and family limited liability companies (see Chapter 5 for a detailed discussion of potential approaches). Using the right techniques and deploying the right entities can make all the difference in terms of being successful in enhancing your wealth for the long run.

2. Wealth transfer

Finding and facilitating the most tax-efficient way to pass assets to your spouse and succeeding generations in ways that meet your wishes.

As detailed in Chapter 6, any estate planning you do should address three categories:

- **People** include you and your spouse, your children, your grandchildren, and your other relatives. Ask yourself: What do you want for them? What do they want for themselves? How involved are they in the process? People may also involve identifying and working with a number of professionals and organizations.

- **Property** includes your wealth and assets of all kinds—money, investments, real property, personal property, retirement funds and potential inheritances—both presently and prospectively owned.
- **Process** refers to developing an estate plan to make optimum use of the legal entities (such as trusts), techniques and management initiatives that are most likely to effectively achieve your long-term wishes. Process also involves determining who will be responsible for executing the plan for the long run.

3. Wealth protection

Guarding your wealth against catastrophic loss, potential creditors, litigants and identity thieves.

Today, the affluent tend to share four main security and protection concerns:

- Protection concerns for self and loved ones
- Protection concerns about confidential information
- Protection concerns about financial assets
- Protection concerns about property

There are two ways you can protect your wealth. First, you can mitigate risk. This means taking actions that will minimize your exposure to a risk and, should that risk occur, reduce its impact. As detailed in Chapter 7, there are many ways to mitigate risk in each of the four categories above, depending on the situation. Second, you can transfer risk, or shift it away from yourself and to another party. The most common means to transfer risk is to purchase insurance. Chapter 7 also describes many ways to transfer the risk your wealth faces.

4. Charitable giving

Fulfilling your charitable goals in the most impactful way possible.

Proper planning can help you make the most of each dollar you give and maximize your philanthropic impact in a number of ways:

- Leverage financial benefits
- Fully support your values
- Focus and streamline your giving
- Involve family
- Maximize tax benefits

To create an effective charitable giving plan, consider the following steps from Chapter 8:

- **Formulate your goals.** When your giving reflects your deepest values and interests, philanthropy becomes powerful and profoundly rewarding. What do you care about most? What values do you want to convey with your giving? And what do you hope your giving will ultimately achieve?
- **Decide where to give.** Ask people who are active in the causes that interest you for recommendations, and talk to friends and colleagues who share your charitable interests about the organizations they support. Once you have a list of candidates, confirm by looking at the mission statement of each that they support your goals. Then conduct further research to verify that they will use your contributions effectively and efficiently.
- **Decide when to give.** Typically, individuals make contributions in one or more of the following three ways: annual giving (regular, ongoing contributions are usually tied to the tax year), legacy giving (which may involve a simple will bequest or more complex vehicles) and giving in response to a crisis.

- **Decide what to give.** Depending on your situation and the tax rules in effect at any given time, you might choose to donate cash, appreciated stock and/or tangible property. You might also decide to give your time and expertise by volunteering for one or more charities.

Step 4. Build and manage your team of specialists

Relationship management is the third component of the Wealth Management Edge process. It is all about getting the help that will allow you to do a great job at successfully managing your entire financial life over time by building, managing and working with the right team of financial specialists—professionals who have deep knowledge across the range of specialties that you require.

Having the right team in place is a key driver of financial success for today's affluent families. Many of the tasks required to build and maintain a strong financial future for yourself and your family are complex and time-consuming—they demand a high level of knowledge and focus. Just as important is the fact that no one person—not even one of the best financial professionals working today—can be a true specialist in every single one of the investment and advanced planning approaches that today's affluent families require. By surrounding yourself with a group of financial professionals, you can ensure that you benefit from the best advice possible in each area.

If you choose to work with a financial advisor as your wealth manager, it is important to select one who has a team of specialists capable of providing the advice you need. However, working with the right team of specialists is a key step you must take regardless of whether or not you work with a financial advisor. Even the biggest "do it yourselfers" need to find and work with specialists.

The core members of your team should include the following professionals:

- **A private client lawyer** who can address the types of tax, estate planning and legal needs detailed in this book.

- **An accountant** to make specific recommendations to mitigate income and other taxes.
- **A life insurance professional** to identify and structure a plan that leverages the entire range of life insurance benefits, such as those that have been discussed throughout this book.

If you build and manage your own team, your best sources for finding potential specialists for your team are most likely your friends and associates—other like-minded people you know well and trust and who have goals and needs similar to yours. In addition, the specialists you work with often have professional networks of their own that they can refer you to.

Alternatively, you can work with a wealth manager who can provide you with access to the resources you need and who can build and manage the team on your behalf. For example, wealth managers who use the Wealth Management Edge process focus primarily on helping investors with their investment consulting and wealth preservation needs. They develop relationships with private client lawyers, accountants, insurance specialists and other financial professionals and work with them regularly to meet their clients' advanced planning needs.

Regardless of which approach you take, remember from Chapter 9 that you will want to evaluate each professional on how well he or she demonstrates the six traits that most contribute to clients' satisfaction with their financial advisors:

1. Character
2. Chemistry
3. Caring
4. Competence
5. Cost-effective
6. Consultative

PUTTING IT ALL TOGETHER

Best of success to you and your family

The next step is yours to take. You can continue to manage your financial life as you have been doing to this point, or you can begin to use the Wealth Management Edge process—either entirely on your own or in partnership with a financial advisor who follows the tenets of the Wealth Management Edge approach.

If you continue on as you have been, it's entirely possible that you will enjoy much financial and personal success. There are lots of ways to manage wealth, and many of them can be quite effective.

But what I can tell you with the utmost confidence and certainty is this: If you use the Wealth Management Edge approach detailed in this book, you will put yourself in the best possible position to make informed decisions about your wealth so you can live the type of life that you truly want. In my more than 30 years of working with investors and the financial advisors who serve them, I have never seen a more powerful, more effective way for families to enhance, protect and transfer wealth.

Now that you have come to the end of this book, take some time to think about your most important goals for yourself—those things you want to achieve that will make your life deeply meaningful. Think about the people around you whom you value—who might include your spouse, your children and your extended family. And think about the people, groups or causes that you most want to support and help do good work.

The fact is, the wealth you build over your lifetime can have a huge impact on so many people—from you and the people you share your life with every day to the world at large. When you think about it from that perspective, I think you will agree that one of your biggest responsibilities is to be a good steward of that wealth by making the smartest possible choices about how you save, invest, spend and protect it, and pass it on.

Ultimately, that is what the Wealth Management Edge is all about—helping you make the smartest choices about your wealth so that it can do the maximum good for you and everyone you care about.

I wish you and your family the best as you build a lifetime of financial success and achieve all that is truly important to you.